Verona &
Lake Garda

Shona Main, Lara Dunston
& Terry Carter

Credits

Footprint credits

Editor: Alan Murphy
Production and layout: Jen Haddington
Maps: Gail Townsley

Managing Director: Andy Riddle
Content Director: Patrick Dawson
Publisher: Alan Murphy
Publishing Managers: Felicity Laughton,
Jo Williams, Nicola Gibbs
Marketing and Partnerships Director:
Liz Harper
Marketing Executive: Liz Eyles
Trade Product Manager: Diane McEntee
Account Managers: Paul Bew, Tania Ross
Advertising: Renu Sibal, Elizabeth Taylor
Finance: Phil Walsh

Photography credits
Front cover: Federico Donatini/Dreamstime
Back cover: Fabrizio Argonauta/Dreamstime

Printed in Great Britain by CPI Antony Rowe,
Chippenham, Wiltshire

Every effort has been made to ensure that
the facts in this guidebook are accurate.
However, travellers should still obtain advice
from consulates, airlines, etc about travel
and visa requirements before travelling.
The authors and publishers cannot
accept responsibility for any loss, injury or
inconvenience however caused.

Publishing information
Footprint *Focus Verona & Lake Garda*
1st edition
© Footprint Handbooks Ltd
April 2012

ISBN: 978 1 908206 55 8
CIP DATA: A catalogue record for this book is
available from the British Library

® Footprint Handbooks and the Footprint
mark are a registered trademark of Footprint
Handbooks Ltd

Published by Footprints
6 Riverside Court
Lower Bristol Road
Bath BA2 3DZ, UK
T +44 (0)1225 469141
F +44 (0)1225 469461
footprinttravelguides.com

Distributed in the USA by Globe Pequot
Press, Guilford, Connecticut

The content of Footprint *Focus Verona & Lake
Garda* has been extracted from Footprint's
Venice & Veneto, which was researched and
written by Shona Main, and Footprint's
Italian Lakes, which was researched and
written by Lara Dunston and Terry Carter.

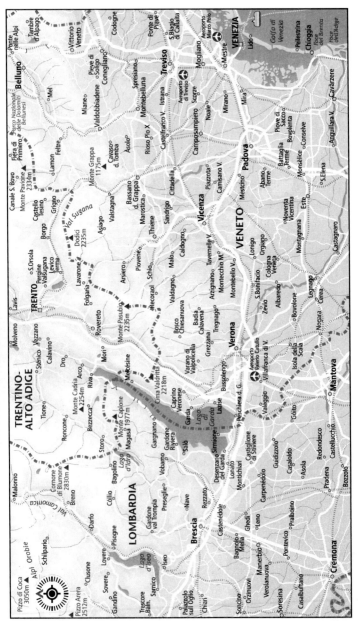

The regions in which Verona and Lake Garda lie are some of the wealthiest in Italy and the richest in diversity.

The east coast of shimmering Lake Garda, the Roman city of Verona and the Palladian architecture of Vicenza reside in the Alpine foothills of prosperous Veneto whilst the dramatic west coast of Garda, the post-industrial, culturally thriving city of Brescia, and low-lying Cremona and Mantua are in the manufacturing and agricultural powerhouse of Lombardy.

The Roman ruins of Verona, Sirmione and Brescia show that this area was always built on ambition and power-struggles. Fragmented into often warring city states, the North of Italy came together briefly in the 12th century to see off the imperialist plans of the German Holy Roman Emperor Frederick I (aka Barbarossa or 'red beard'). However, once the external enemy was dealt with the unity broke and each city went back behind their fortifications where they seethed and plotted against each other.

Ruling dynasties left dazzling cultural legacies: the Scaligeri of Verona, the Gonzaga of Matua and the Milanese Visconti and Sforza in Cremona. Boundaries and displays of wealth were paramount: walls and Castelli showed strength whilst churches, buildings and art showed their greatness.

When the maritime might of the Republic of Venice turned to terrafirma affairs Brescia, Verona and other hinterlands fell under their control. After Napoleon crushed the Venetian state, the Austrians moved in but only until 1870 when Italy was unified by Garibaldi and everyone became an Italian.

Once the playground of the monied and the Fascisti, Garda is now invaded each weekend by the hot and sticky Bresciani and Veronesi who pine for fresh-air pursuits and cooler nights in their family villas.

Sun worshippers, shopaholics, outdoor types, foodies, wine buffs or art and history lovers: there's something and everything here for all visitors.

Planning your trip

Places to visit in Verona and Lake Garda

Verona
Verona is suspended in fiction by an Englishman who had never visited and mobbed by tourists who come to see the balcony of a young girl who never existed. But the romance and drama of Verona is very real. The Roman legacy of its astonishing amphitheatre, *teatro* and other ruins under your feet has been complemented over the years by monumental churches and gracious palazzi to create a perfect stage set for an enchanting stay. Around Verona, the western Veneto is characterized by vineyards that cling to every hill and patch of fertile soil, fed by the Alpine waters of the Adige and its tributaries.

Vicenza and around
Back down on the plains, on the route that links Venice with Milan, lies Vicenza. One of the wealthiest cities in Italy, it is also one of the smallest and the most architecturally rich. The handiwork of Palladio is all around you, from the palazzi and public buildings in the city centre to the villas in the surrounding countryside, where La Rotonda, considered his most perfect tribute to the principles of proportion, symmetry and pleasure, sits in absolute harmony with the landscape. To the north of Vicenza lies Bassano del Grappa, a town made famous by the WWI heroics of Italy's elite mountain soldiers, the Alpini. Visitors will not fail to be lifted by their bravery, and by the locally brewed Grappa, an eye-watering firewater if ever there was. Nearby the fortifications of medieval Marostica make a stunning stage set for its famous game of human chess.

Lake Garda
The largest of the lakes, Lake Garda has a bit of everything for everyone. Its faded charm, historic hotels and Michelin-starred restaurants appeal to an older, more affluent traveller, while its water sports, good beaches and theme parks attract families en masse throughout the summer months. Gardone Riviera and Salò are the places to visit for refined hotels and restaurants and loads of lakeside ambience, while Sirmione's traffic-free streets, striking castle and Roman ruins attract the sightseers, and Riva del Garda's windsurfing is a magnet for sporty types. Not far away, low-key Lake Iseo, with its picturesque waterside promenades, pretty squares and plenty of camping opportunities, is the least tourist-driven of the lakes, making it the most alluring for some.

Towns of the Po Valley
Brescia, **Cremona** and **Mantua** are all conveniently located near the lakes, making great bases for day trips to the lakes when accommodation is hard to come by during summer or when hotels are closed during the cooler months. The closest town to Lake Iseo, Brescia is a hidden gem with elegant *palazzi* (palaces/mansions) and lovely piazzas that rarely get crowded with tourists, even during the peak summer period, and yet it's conveniently located on the Milan-Verona train line. The small laid-back Lombardy cities of Cremona and Mantua ooze atmosphere and charm; both are connected to Milan, Brescia, Bergamo and Verona by train and freeway.

Best of Verona and Lake Garda

Arena Verona's Roman amphitheatre is in amazingly good condition, despite having been built 2000 years ago. It is now the setting for Verona's famous opera season; a performance here is a spectacle never forgotten. Page 21.

Teatro Romano and Museo Archeologico Verona's Roman theatre is still used as a performance venue and has held on to its ancient allure. The Museo, housed high on a hill in the former convent of San Girolamo, offers the most majestic views of the Teatro and of Verona itself. Page 26.

Teatro Olimpico Palladio may have designed this semi-circular tiered theatre in Vicenza but it is Vincenzo Scamozzi's stage set that draws gasps of wonder. Still in use, it is the only surviving Renaissance theatre in Italy. Page 37.

La Rotonda This is considered by many architects to be the perfect building. Palladio himself took great pride in the way the landscape, materials, location, symmetry and mathematical precision came together in such beauteous harmony. Page 42.

Brescia The combination of Roman ruins and fascisti architecture provides a stirring backdrop to one of Italy's most modern-minded multicultural cities. Don't miss the Museo di Santa Giulia, a sprawling many-layered complex of ruins, atefacts, churches and art. Page 70.

Cremona Celebrated as the birthplace of serious violin making and home to the famous *Stradivari*, the atmospheric city of Cremona with its impressive Museo Stradivariano and Collezione Gli Archi, its hundreds of violin-makers' workshops, and the sound of music in the streets, is equally as rewarding for ordinary travellers as it is for music aficionados. Page 76.

Getting to Verona and Lake Garda

Air

From UK and Ireland British Airways have daily flights to Verona Valerio Catullo from Gatwick. Direct flights to Venice Marco Polo leave from London Heathrow (**bmi**, **British Airways**); Manchester and East Midlands (**easyJet**) and London Gatwick (**easyJet**, **British Airways**). During the summer months there are also daily flights from Edinburgh and Leeds (**Jet2**). **Ryanair** have flights to Treviso from Dublin and London Stansted.

From North America Alitalia and Delta fly directly from New York to Venice Marco Polo (transit time around 12 hours). **Air France**, **Air Canada**, **Alitalia**, **British Airways**, **Delta** and **KLM** fly direct from Canada to Venice Marco Polo.

From rest of Europe There are direct flights to Venice Marco Polo from many European cities including Berlin, Amsterdam, Paris and Stockholm. Carriers include **Air France**, **Alitalia**, **Austrian**, **easyJet**, **Lufthansa** and **Swiss**. **Ryanair** connect a number of European cities with Treviso and **Transavia** fly daily from Amsterdam to Treviso and Verona.

Airport information

Venice Marco Polo ① *T041-260 9260, www.veniceairport.it*, lies on the mainland due north of Venice. The arrivals hall has an **APT di Venezia tourist office** ① *T041-541 5887, daily 0900-1800*, and a number of car hire companies, including **Avis** ① *T041-541 5030, avis. co.uk*, **Europcar** ① *T041-541 5654, europcar.co.uk*, and **Hertz** ① *T041-541 6075, hertz.com*; all are open daily 0800-2400.

The airport is 19 km by road and 8 km by sea from the city centre. A waterbus service runs roughly every half hour from the airport with Linea Blue and Linea Arancio, taking you to stops nearby the train station, Venice Santa Lucia FS (around €14 per person); buy tickets at the **Alilaguna** (alilaguna.it) stand in arrivals. Water taxis are convenient but are much more expensive (up to €100). Bus services go to piazzale Roma every 30 minutes: for the ATVO Aerobus (€9 return or €5 single) or the cheap and cheerful ACTV (€1.30 single).

Brescia, Verona, Vicenza and the train stations that connect to those around Lake Garda all sit on the main Venice to Milan line. Connections to Mantova are available from Verona and Cremona from Brescia.

Treviso ① *T042-231 5131, trevisoairport.it*, is a **Ryanair** hub, located 6 km from Treviso city centre and 34 km from Venice. The arrivals hall has a small **Treviso IAT tourist office** ① *T0422-263282, Mon and Fri 0830-1400 and 1630-1700, Tue and Thu 1430-1700, Wed 0800-1030 and 1330-1900, Sat 1430-1900 and 2000-2230*, and a number of car hire companies, including **Avis** ① *T0422-433351, avis.co.uk*, and **Hertz** ① *T0422-297027, hertz.com*. **ATVO** (atvo.it) runs a bus service from the airport to piazzale Roma in Venice (€7 single, €13 return with 7-day validity, 1 hour). Alternatively, take bus no.6 to Treviso Centrale train station (€1.20 at airport, €2.50 on board, 15-20 minutes) from where there are frequent rail connections to Brescia, Verona, Vicenza and connecting towns.

Verona Valerio Cattullo ① *T045-809 5666, aeroportoverona.it*, is 12 km south of Verona. The arrivals hall has a **Verona APT tourist office** ① *T045-861 9163, Apr-Nov Mon-Sat 0900-1800, Sun 0900-1500, Dec-Mar Mon-Sat 0900-1600, Sun 0900-1500*. Car hire is available from **Avis** ① *T045-987571, avis.co.uk*, and **Hertz** ① *T045-861 9042, hertz.com*. **APTV** (aptv.it) run the Aerobus service to and from the train and bus station at porta Nuova every 20 minutes (€6, 15 minutes). Taxis are available just outside the arrivals hall and cost around €25 into the *centro storico*.

Rail

It is possible to travel to the region by rail from the UK by taking the **Eurostar** (eurostar.com) service from London St Pancras to Paris Gare du Nord (from £59 return, 2 hours 25 minutes) and then crossing Paris to the Gare de Bercy to catch a direct overnight sleeper (from £60 return) to Venice Santa Lucia. The train stops at Brescia, Verona and Vicenza en route. Daytime travel is also possible but you'll have to spend a night in either Paris, Milan or Geneva. Buy tickets through **Rail Europe** ① *T0870-584 8848, raileurope.co.uk, raileurope.com*, or **SNCF** (voyages-sncf.com). For comprehensive information on rail travel throughout Europe, consult seat61.com.

For luxury, there's the **Venice Simplon-Orient Express** (orient-express.com), which runs from London Victoria to Venice Santa Lucia, via Paris, Innsbruck and Verona, between March and November, with departures on Thursday and Sunday mornings; it arrives in Venice the following evening. Prices start at £1530 for a one-way trip or £2300 for a return.

The Hotel Cipriani is owned by the same company and offers special deals for Orient Express travellers.

Road

Car If you're up for the 1500 km journey and can afford the petrol, you could drive from the UK to Venice. The journey will take a leisurely 24 hours (if you're lucky). The most popular route is down through France, entering Italy through the Mont Blanc tunnel just north of Turin, then on to Milan, where you join the A4 across northern Italy to Brescia, Lake Garda and Verona.

Bus/coach Eurolines ① *T041-538 2118, eurolines.com*, run long-distance coaches from all over Europe to piazzale Roma in Venice and to the bus stations in Brescia, Vicenza and Verona. From London to Venice or Verona takes just over 30 hours and costs from £50 for a one-way ticket booked 30 days in advance.

Transport in Verona and Lake Garda

Rail

Italy's hugely extensive, efficient and affordable rail network is the best way to get around the country on a city-based trip. It is served by air-conditioned and splendid Eurostar Italia trains (ES); direct and convenient InterCity trains (IC), and the slightly less regular and slower Regional trains (REG). All can be booked at trenitalia.com; booking is advised for Eurostar Italia and InterCity services.

Ticket prices are sure to be a pleasant surprise: a single from Verona to Venice is €15 for the Intercity or €5 for the Regionale; Verona ot Mantova is just €3.30. As well as standard fares there are also cheaper Amica fares, available in advance, and first class tickets, which are not that much more expensive. Booking and buying tickets at the counter in a station usually involves a long wait so look for the ticket-dispensing machines. These take cash and/or credit or debit cards, have a number of language functions and offer all the options, prices and timings. Remember, you must validate train tickets at the yellow stamping machines before boarding, although on many Italian trains it is possible to travel 'ticketless' by quoting a booking reference to the conductor instead. In general, it's cheaper and more convenient to book individual journeys online or to buy the ticket at the station than it is to buy a pass for multiple journeys; Eurostar Italia and InterCity services often have a surcharge that makes rail passes less cost-effective.

The main rail route through Veneto runs from Venice Santa Lucia to Milan via Mestre, Vicenza Centrale (1 hour) and Verona Porta Nuova (1½ hours). This is well served by Eurostar and InterCity trains with one every hour or so. Slower, regional trains also operate on this route and are occasionally the most suitable option, especially on Sundays or at night. Train travel to Lake Garda is from Brescia or Verona, with stops at Peschiera del Garda and Desenzano. You can get a train to Cremona from Brescia and one to Manotva from Verona. **Trenitalia** ① *T89-20-21, trenitalia.it*, has details of all routes.

Road

Car EU nationals taking their own car into Italy need to have an International Insurance Certificate (also known as a *Carta Verde*) and a valid national or EU licence. Those holding a non-EU licence need to take an International Driving Permit with them.

Speed limits are 130 km per hour on *autostrade* (motorways), 110 km per hour on dual carriageways and 50 km per hour in towns. (Limits are 20 km per hour lower on motorways and dual carriageways when the road is wet.) *Autostrade* are toll roads, so keep cash in the car as a back-up even though you can use credit cards on the blue 'viacard' gates. **Autostrade** ① *autostrade.it*, provides information on motorways in Italy and **Automobile Club d'Italia** ① *T06-491115*, *aci.it*, provides general driving information. It also offers roadside assistance with English-speaking operators on T803116.

Key routes in the region include the **A4**, which runs across southern Veneto, linking Milan with Brescia, Desenzano (with the SS1 up the west side of Gardo to Salo and then up the SS45 to Limone) and Peschiera del Garda (where the SS249 takes you up the east side). The A4 then continues along to Verona and Vicenza, before continuing east to Venice. The A22 from Verona takes you to Mantua. Cremona is linked to Mantua by the SS10 and to Brescia by the A21.

Be aware that there are restrictions on driving in historic city centres, indicated by signs with black letters ZTL (*zona a traffico limitato*) on a yellow background. If you ignore these signs, you are liable for a fine. Parking is usually available outside the *centro storico* for €2-5 an hour depending on the location. City hotels will either provide parking for guests or will be able to direct you to the nearest car park.

On-the-spot fines for minor traffic offences are in operation; typically they range from €150 to €250 (always get a receipt). Note the following legal requirements: the use of mobile telephones while driving is not permitted; front and rear seatbelts must be worn, if fitted; children under 1.5 m may only travel in the back of the car. Italy has very strict laws on drink driving: the legal limit is 0.5g per litre of blood compared to the UK's 0.8g. If your car breaks down on the carriageway, you must display an emergency triangle and wear a reflective jacket in poor visibility. Car hire companies should provide both of these, but check the boot when you pick up your car.

Car hire Car hire is available at all three international airports in the region. You are advised to book your hire car before you arrive in the country, especially at busy times of year. Car hire comparison websites and agents are a good place to start a search for the best deals: try avis.com, europcar.co.uk and hertz.co.uk. Check what each hire company requires from you: some companies will ask for an International Driving Licence alongside your normal driving licence; others are content with an EU licence. You will also need a credit card, so, if you book ahead, make sure that the named credit card holder is the same as the person renting and driving the car. Most companies have a lower age limit of 21 years, with a young driver surcharge for those under 25, and require that you've held your licence for at least a year. Confirm the company's insurance and damage waiver policies and keep all your documents with you when you drive.

Bicycle If your thighs are up to it and you are confident on roads populated with fast and crazy drivers, cycling around the Garda and the Po Valley can be memorable. Arm yourself with a good map: the Edizioni Multigraphic's *Carta Turistica Stradale* (1:50,000) has enough detail for most cyclists, while the 1:25,000 version is useful for those who like to go off road. Bikes are allowed on many train services: check out trenitalia.it for more information. The **European Cycling Federation** (ecf.com) promotes cycling in Europe and has some good advice as well as links to companies that provide biking tours in the region.

Bus/coach With trains so fast, cheap and efficient, it is only in the more rural areas that buses provide a useful service. Check with the local tourist information office to confirm times and pick-up points, as well as to find out where to buy tickets (it's often a nearby newsagent or tobacconists). Brescia, Cremon, Mantua, Vicenza and Verona all have city bus services. Again, you can buy tickets from newsagents, tobacconists (look for a big T sign) and even some cafés: if you intend to make a number of journeys, buy a stash of tickets at once. Always remember to validate your ticket when you board by stamping it in the machine located at the front and sometimes also at the back of the bus.

Where to stay in Verona and Lake Garda

There's a variety of accommodation on offer in the region, including B&Bs, *agriturismo* and apart-hotels. It's always easiest to stay in or close to the *centro storico* of a city, but those who don't mind taking buses or taxis or who are renting a car will find some great villas amongst the vineyards and cypress trees on the outskirts or beyond.

On arrival in Italy you used to have to register with the local police station. Now, when you check in (be it at a hotel, B&B or even to pick up apartment keys), hand over your passport and staff will take down the details to pass on to the police.

On paper, Italy has a star classification system akin to other European countries, but the reality on the ground doesn't quite reflect the ratings. Amenities that have been listed often don't exist or have only earned them a rating due to mere technical compliance (such as the dimensions of the bar or dining area). The hotels are graded from one- to five-star deluxe, but a well-run, well-positioned three-star can often offer a better experience than a five-star filled with self-absorbed staff or a position on the outskirts of the town centre.

In one- and two-star hotels (sometimes called *pensioni*) you often have to share bathrooms, but some of these properties can be full of atmosphere, with genial hosts. The three-star options almost always have an en suite bathroom and air conditioning – strongly recommended for the sticky summers. If a place is described as an *albergo*, these days it simply means a hotel and it can have any star rating. Similarly with a *locanda*, which traditionally referred to an inn or a restaurant with rooms. A bed and breakfast can simply be a room in someone's residence (for better or worse) or can mean a charming stay in a lovely cottage or cabin where only breakfast is served.

While *agriturismi* – that is, rural accommodation or rooms on a working farm or vineyard – are hugely popular in regions such as Tuscany and Umbria, the trend has been slower to take off in the lakes area where the grand hotel experience dominates. If you're determined to seek out such experiences in this part of Italy, do your research carefully as many properties are based on a great idea but the experiences are poorly executed; see loveitaly.co.uk and agriturist.it for some of the best examples.

If you're intending to spend more than a week in one place and you're not planning on bugging the concierge every 15 minutes for directions or restaurant bookings, seriously consider renting an apartment for your stay. Not only will you save money if you're looking at anything from mid range or above, but shopping for groceries at the local markets and living like a local in a city that you want to get to know better can be just as enjoyable and rewarding as seeing a major attraction you've always dreamt of visiting.

Price codes

Where to stay

€€€€ over €300   €€€ €200-300

€€ €100-200   € under €100

Prices refer to the cost of two people sharing a double room in the high season.

Restaurants

€€€€ over €40   €€€ €30-40

€€ €20-30   € under €20

Prices refer to the average cost of a two-course meal for one person, including drinks and service charge.

Food and drink in Verona and Lake Garda

What to eat

Ease of transportation means that fresh seafood is popular and readily available throughout the Veneto, but the further inland you go the less of it is to be found in traditional regional cooking. In winter particularly, dried fish was traditionally used, as in the Vicentine dish of *baccalà alla Vicentina* (dried cod braised with onions, milk and cheese).

In Verona, popular dishes include meat stewed with Amarone wine and *bollito con la peará* (boiled meat with bread sauce). Diners from the UK and US may be perturbed to find *caval/cavallo* (horse) and *asino* (donkey) on the menu in Veneto. It is often served shredded with olive oil and balsamic vinegar (*sfilacci di cavallo*), cooked in a stew (*pastissada de caval*) or in a pasta sauce (*bigoli con ragu d'asino*).

Regional pasta varieties include *bigoli* (fat spaghetti, often wholewheat) and varieties of tortelloni, including the pumpkin-filled sort (*tortelli di zucca*) from Mantua. Veneto is where gnocchi (small potato dumplings) were invented and, in the mountainous parts of the region, you'll find *canederli*, a super-sized version. Two of Italy's most heart-warming dishes also originated here: polenta (served as a maize porridge or left to harden, then fried) and risotto: try *risotto dell'Amarone* in Verona.

The quality of the vegetables in Veneto is splendid: a simple plate of *melanzane e zucchini grigliate* (grilled aubergine and courgette) served with a lump of *mezzanello di monte* (a local cheese) is a dream dish. And if you're in Bassano del Grappa in May, try the ghostly white fingers of its famous *asparago bianco* (white asparagus).

Where to eat

Italians famously love to eat and to eat out and there is a range of venues to cater for their needs. Technically and historically *ristoranti* are posher than *trattorie*, while *osterie* are primarily wine bars. However, you'll soon notice that these names are little help in telling you the price or salubriousness of an establishment.

When to eat

Colazione Breakfast usually consists of nothing more than a cappuccino and a *cornetto* – a pastry filled with *crema* (custard), marmalade or Nutella – and is consumed on the go in a bar, any time from 0600 until the *cornetti* run out. Larger hotels tend to offer a buffet breakfast of eggs, cheese, ham, cakes, yoghurts, etc.

Pranzo Lunch is served between 1000 and 1400 but can go on for a bit longer than that. The sequence of an Italian menu is: *antipasta* (starter); *primo piatto* (first dish), which is usually pasta or risotto; *secondo piatto* (second dish), which is meat- or fish-based and often served with or before *contorni* (vegetables) or salad, and, finally, *dolce* (dessert). Don't think for a minute you have to order all of this: you can have as much or as little as you want. Likewise, you can order a glass of wine, instead of a whole bottle, or just have water or even beer (in some places). Prices are reasonable; you can have a *primo*, a *secondo* and some wine for €10 in **Pane e Vino** in Verona, for example, see page 30.

Cena Dinner is served between 1900 and 2200, although some places will stop taking orders at 2100. It follows the same format as lunch and should cost the same.

Note The cover charge should be stated on the menu and can be anything from €2 to €8. There might also be a service charge of 10%. If you're on a tight budget, it's wise to calculate the real cost of your meal, including charges, before you sit down.

The best wines of Veneto

Valpolicella This red wine has a poor reputation in Britain but is enjoyed by those in the region and, at its best, by wine lovers in the know. It's a soft, cherryish, easy-to-drink wine made from Corvina, Rondinella and Molinara varieties that are grown in the Negrar and Adige valleys. There are two types: Superiore, which has aged for a year, and Classico, which comes from the Valpolicella area north of Verona. Top producers include Allegrini, Tedeschi and Quintarelli.

Recioto della Valpolicella The *rece* (ears) are the grapes on the outside of a bunch and are the ripest and most mature. They are laid out on mats to dry before being used to make this sweet, rich wine.

Amarone This is essentially Recioto della Valpolicella that has undergone at least 25 months (but often five to ten years) fermentation in oak barrels to produce a dry but robust dark red wine, reminiscent of bitter chocolate. Amarone is considered by many to be the best wine from the Veneto.

Bardolino Grown on the eastern shores of Lago di Garda, Bardolino uses the same grapes as Valpolicella but in different proportions: less Corvina and more Rondinella. It can include a small percentage of local varieties, too. There's a Superiore (aged for at least one year and with a higher alcohol content); a rosé, known as Bardolino Chiaretto, which has a shorter fermentation period; a lightly sparkling *frizzante*, and a *novello* (similar to a Beaujolais Nouveau).

Soave Hailing from an area east of Verona, this white wine is made from Garganega and Trebbiano grapes. British wine snobs are rather sniffy about it, but it is celebrated by locals who love its freshness. There's a *reciot* version made in the same way as Recioto della Valpolicella.

Prosecco Grown and produced in the area between Conegliano and Valdobbiadene, just north of Treviso, this white wine comes in three varieties: dry sparkling (*spumante*), semi-sparkling (*frizzante*) and still. It is served by the glass in all bars (should be no more than €4 depending where you are) and can also be mixed to create classic cocktails. A Bellini, inspired by the pinky hue from a Bellini painting, is prosecco mixed with white peach purée and a spot of raspberry juice.

Ordering coffee

If you ask for '*un caffè*' in Italy, you will be served an espresso in a very small cup. It's strong in taste with a creamy froth known as *crema*. Some suggest that ordering a cappuccino after 1030 in the morning will earn derisive looks from the locals. Poppycock! Order whichever coffee you want, whenever you want; as long as you pay, they'll not care a jot.

caffè Americano weaker coffee made with more hot water.
caffè latte coffee made with lots of hot milk and a touch of foam on top.
cappuccino espresso with hot milk and a thick foamy top.
cappuccino chiaro weaker cappuccino but not yet a caffè latte.
cappuccino scuro strong cappuccino.
corretto espresso 'corrected' by a slug of grappa.
doppio double espresso.
latte macchiato steamed milk 'marked' with a shot of espresso.
lungo longer, weaker coffee made with more hot water.
macchiato espresso 'marked' with steamed milk on top.
ristretto strong espresso made with less water.

Festivals in Verona and Lake Garda

January
Carnevale di Verona Dating back to the 1500s, this is one of the oldest celebrations in Italy. It recounts a local nobleman's gift of gnocchi (pasta dumplings made of flour and potato) to the people after the price of flour became exorbitant following the plague. Taking place in late January or early February, it features extravagant costumes, loud bands, lively parades and some unusually exuberant behaviour from the locals – said to be caused by the wind.

April
Easter Celebrations, including processions and hugely popular church services, take place throughout Italy.
Vinitaly The biggest wine fair in the country runs for five days in Verona (vinitaly.com).

May
Le Piazze dei Sapori Verona's 'Squares of Flavours' features several days of celebrating local produce and wines, with plenty of tastings, music and dance.
Mille Miglia While it's no longer a serious car race as such, Brescia's historic road race offers an opportunity to witness the sights and sounds of some wonderful Italian classic cars such as Alfa Romeos and Ferraris.

June
Festival Lirico all'Arena di
Verona Verona's opera season begins in late June and runs until September at the Arena. Rotating classics, including *Aida* and often *Tosca*, are played out in this most awesome of venues.
Festival Shakespeariano The Shakespeare festival in Verona starts late in the month and runs until early August with performances in the Teatro Olimpico.
Garda Jazz Festival This summer jazz festival, running over a couple of weeks in Riva del Garda, features some great jazz by Italy's often-underrated jazz players (gardajazz.com).

July

Sognando Shakespeare A celebration of the Bard and his infatuation with the city of fair Verona. During July and August, events include dance and jazz performances, and, of course, Shakespeare's plays (some in English).

August

Ferragosto (15th) The Feast of the Assumption is celebrated all over the country with gusto – by doing as little as possible and eating as much as possible. For some it's the start of the summer holiday, for others it's the halfway mark.

Rustico Medioevo Held in the second week of August, this is a charming medieval dance and folkloric festival at Canale di Tenno, Riva del Garda (rusticomedioevo.com).

September

Partita a Scacchi (second Sunday In even years) This faux medieval festival is held in the town of Marostica and involves residents dressing up in costume to watch a game of human chess on Marostica's main piazza.

October

Notte Bianca A new festival of all night access to art galleries to celebrate the city's burgeoning reputation as a centre for edgy contemporary art.

November

Tutti Santi (1st) All Saints' Day is a public holiday with numerous religious celebrations. Italians traditionally enjoy a harvest feast, give presents to their children, and attend a special mass.

December

Stalls of Santa Lucia (13th) For several days before and after the Feast of Santa Lucia, Verona's piazza Bra is home to a lively Christmas fair with toys, gastronomic delights, and weird and wonderful bits and pieces.

Essentials A-Z

Customs and immigration
UK and EU citizens do not need a visa but will need a valid passport to enter Italy. A standard tourist visa for those from outside the EU is valid for up to 90 days.

Disabled travellers
Northern Italy is beginning to adapt to the needs of disabled travellers but access can still be very difficult due to the age of many historic buildings or the lack of careful planning. For more details and advice, contact a specialist agency before departure, such as **Accessible Italy** (accessibleitaly.com) or **Society for Accessible Travel and Hospitality** (sath.org).

Emergencies
Ambulance T118; **Fire service** T115; **Police** T112 (with English-speaking operators), T113 (*carabinieri*); **Roadside assistance** T116.

Etiquette
Bella figura – projecting a good image – is important to Italians. Take note of public notices about conduct: sitting on steps or eating and drinking in certain historic areas is not allowed. Covering arms and legs is necessary for admission into some churches – in rare cases even shorts are not permitted. Punctuality, like queuing, is an alien concept in Italy, so be prepared to wait on occasion but not necessarily in line or order.

Families
The family is highly regarded in Italy and children are well treated (not to say indulged), particularly in restaurants (although more expensive restaurants may not admit children). Note that lone parents or adults accompanying children of a different surname may sometimes need proof of guardianship before taking children in and out of Italy; contact your Italian embassy for current details (Italian embassy in London, T020-7312 2200).

Health
Comprehensive medical insurance is strongly recommended for all travellers to Italy. EU citizens should also apply for a free European Health Insurance Card (ehic.org), which replaced the E111 form and offers reduced-cost medical treatment. Late-night pharmacies are identified by a large green cross outside. To obtain the details of the three nearest open pharmacies dial T1100; out-of-hours pharmacies are also advertised in most local newspapers. The accident and emergency department of a hospital is the *pronto soccorso*.

Insurance
Comprehensive travel and medical insurance is strongly recommended for all travellers to Italy. You should check any exclusions, excess and that your policy covers you for all the activities you want to undertake. Keep details of your insurance documents separately. Scanning them, then emailing yourself a copy is a good way to keep the information safe and accessible. Ensure you are fully insured if hiring a car, or, if you're taking your own vehicle, contact your current insurer to check whether you require an international insurance certificate.

Money
The Italian currency is the Euro (€). To change cash or travellers' cheques, look for a *cambio* (exchange office); these tend to give better rates than banks. Banks are open Monday to Friday 0830 to 1300 with some opening again from 1500 to 1600. ATMs that accept major credit and debit cards can be found in every city and town (look around the main piazzas). Many restaurants,

shops, museums and art galleries will take major credit cards but paying directly with debit cards such as Cirrus is less common than in the UK, so having a ready supply of cash may be the most convenient option. You should also keep some cash handy for toll roads, if you're driving.

Allow an absolute minimum of €100 per day per person if eating and sleeping on a budget, sharing accommodation and self-catering, and a minimum of €250 per person per day for a taste of the lakes' luxe life. While accommodation is rarely a bargain here, skipping dinner at the expensive restaurants, and opting for fixed price lunch menus, eating standing at a bar like the locals, and buying snacks from the mouth-watering delicatessens, can keep budget travellers happy. Unless you're taking sporting lessons or hiring a yacht, water-based activities are quite reasonably priced on the lakes.

Opening hours

Shops, churches and a lot of sights close for a long lunch at around 1230 and may not open again until 1600. Many places (particularly clothes shops) are closed on Sunday and/or Monday. Family-run restaurants or bars may also shut for a day during the week. Eateries will often stop serving after lunch (around 1400-1500) and sometimes as early as 2100 in the evenings, so don't expect to be able to order meals at any hour. Finally, the Italian holiday month is August. This means that shops, bars, restaurants and even some sights can be closed for a fortnight or longer. They'll also close for Christmas, New Year and some of January, too.

See Money, above, for details on bank opening hours.

Police

There are five different police forces in Italy. The *carabinieri* are a branch of the army and wear military-style uniforms with a red stripe on their trousers and white sashes. They handle general crime, drug-related crime and public order offences. The *polizia statale* are the national police force and are dressed in blue with a thin purple stripe on their trousers. They are responsible for security on the railways and at airports. The *polizia stradale* handle crime and traffic offences on the motorways and drive blue cars with a white stripe. The *vigili urbani* are local police who wear dark blue (in summer) or black (in winter) uniforms with white hats and direct traffic and issue parking fines in the cities. The *guardia di finanza* wear grey uniforms with grey flat hats or green berets (depending on rank). They are charged with combating counterfeiting, tax evasion and fraud.

In the case of an emergency requiring police attention, dial 113, approach any member of the police or visit a police station (below). If it's a non-emergency, dial 112 for assistance.

Verona: via del Pontiere 32, T045-807 7458.
Vicenza: viale Giuseppe Mazzini 213, T0444-357511.

Post

The Italian post service (poste.it) has a not entirely undeserved reputation for unreliablility, particularly when it comes to handling postcards. You can buy *francobolli* (stamps) at post offices and *tabacchi* (look for T signs). A postcard stamp costs from €0.75 for EU countries and €1.60 for transatlantic destinations; for letters over 20g and parcels, there is a maze of prices and options.

Safety

Statistically, the crime rate in Veneto is lower than in Italy as a whole. However, it is always advisable to take general care at night or when travelling, especially around train stations: don't flaunt your valuables; take only the money you need and don't carry it all in one wallet or pocket. Pick-pockets and bag-cutters operate on public transport, so try not to make it obvious which stop you're getting off at, as it gives potential thieves a timeframe in which to work. Car break-ins are common, so always remove valuables and secure other luggage in the boot. Beware of scams, con artists and sellers of fake goods: you can be fined a considerable amount of money for buying fake designer goods. In general, don't take risks you wouldn't at home.

Telephone
The dialling codes for the main cities are: **Brescia** 030; **Cremona** 0372; **Mantua** 039; **Vicenza** 0444 and **Verona** 045.

You need to use these local codes, even when dialling from within the city or region. The prefix for Italy is +39. You no longer need to drop the initial '0' from the area codes when calling from abroad. For directory enquiries call T12.

Time difference
Italy uses Central European Time, GMT+1.

Tipping
It is increasingly common for service to be included in your bill on top of the cover charge. Where this isn't the case (and, sometimes, even when service is included in the bill), tipping is expected but don't tip unless you are genuinely happy with the service: you do your fellow travellers a disservice if you do. There is no need to tip when buying coffees or drinks but a token of appreciation for good, smiling, grudge-free service, is always appreciated. Having said that, always check your bill before paying it. It's amazing how often extra orders and random prices can appear on your bill in Italy. This goes for shops too.

Tourist information
Nearly every town or village has at least one tourist information office or booth, while the larger cities boast at least two (local and provincial), usually located on the main squares. Most have plenty of information to hand out, as well as having websites, although sometimes these are only in Italian or barely decipherable English. Also check out these helpful websites for more information:

Italian Touring Club: touringclub.it
Italian Tourist Board: italiantouristboard.co.uk
Bed and Breakfasts in Italy: bed-and-breakfast-in-italy.com

Voltage
Italy functions on a 220V mains supply. Plugs are the standard European two-pin variety.

Contents

Footprint features

Verona

Although it's famous for a love story that never happened, Verona is anything but a fake. The Romans, who arrived in 300 BC, had big ambitions for Verona. Their monumental amphitheatre – still in operation today – and Teatro Romano show just how grand their plans were. The Roman Empire may have crumbled but centuries of power struggles, including those involving the Scaligeri family and the Venetian Republic, have left behind a legacy of fine Gothic churches and Romanesque palazzi. These create a beautiful backdrop for a city that enjoys the good life: wine is produced in the surrounding hills and Verona's performing and visual arts scenes draw thousands of visitors each year.

With a population of 260,000, Verona is quite a small city but its wealth and history imbue it with the confidence of a much larger urban centre, and its 20,000 students add youthfulness and an air of excitement. However, it is also politically conservative: the influx of new immigrants and other threats to its way of life are much debated in the city's bars and cafés. Italy is changing fast and Verona isn't happy.

The city is on the main routes to Milan and Venice and has excellent transport links; Lake Garda is only an hour away. The river Adige, rushing down from the Dolomites, swirls round Verona and has created a promontory where the very best of the city is located. This compact centre is easy to explore on foot. There is much to see in Verona but this is also a city for socialising, drinking aperitivi, eating well and shopping better.

Verona

Arena

ⓘ *Piazza Bra, T045-800 5151, arena.it. Jun-Aug (opera season) Tue-Sat 0900-1530, Sep-May Mon 1330-1930, Tue-Sat 0830-1930, €4, €1 children, €3 students and over 65s. For details of opera performances and tickets, see page 31.*

Verona's Roman amphitheatre, the third largest Roman structure in Italy (behind Rome's Colosseum and Capua's amphitheatre) was built around AD 30. Although a major earthquake in 1117 destroyed most of the *ala* (outer ring) and many of its stones have been 'borrowed' over the years to prop up other building projects in the city, it is still in amazingly good nick. The elliptical structure is 139 m long and 110 m wide with 44 tiers of stone seats. For the best view, climb the steps to the top, where only some of the *ala* remains, giving you excellent views of piazza Bra and across the Adige.

The Romans used the Arena for *ludi* (games and shows) that honoured the gods. These could be theatrical performances (*ludi scaenici*), chariot races (*ludi circenses*) or the grisly execution of felons and prisoners of war. (There is no evidence to suggest Christians were slain here.) Up to 30,000 spectators (the entire population of Roman Verona) could watch these events and the clever design allowed this mass of people to flow freely, using the 64 *vomitorio* (entrances) and the *ambulatori* (corridors). Nowadays, due to health and safety regulations, audiences are restricted to 15,000.

In the 16th century a body of learned friends with political backing formed the Arena Conservators, who sought to protect the building and make it safe for use but it wasn't until 1913 that it staged its first opera: Giuseppe's Verdi's *Aida*. Aida remains, perhaps, the most popular opera to be performed here and seems entirely appropriate in such an ancient setting. Other favourites include Puccini's *Tosca*, Bizet's *Carmen* and Rossini's *The Barber of Seville*, all of which suit the scale and extravagance of the Arena and benefit from its amazing acoustics.

During opera season there is always a buzz around the piazza, where the sets for forthcoming productions are stored and gladiators pose for camera-toting tourists for a Euro or two. You can visit during the day as a sightseer but the best way to see and experience the Arena is to attend an opera. These shows are spectacular, with exaggerated colours, lights, costumes and drama. The crowd is pretty eye-popping too: the local glitterati sit on plush red chairs at the front and totter off in their Gucci heels for a prosecco during the interval, while up at the back, families with children spread out on the marble seats (or steps, rather) and tuck into picnics. You can hire cushions and buy drinks from cheeky-chappy coke sellers with an eye for the ladies. When you enter the Arena you will be given a candle or *mocoleto* with a card to catch the hot wax. Come the moment of darkness, everyone lights their candle and the whole arena twinkles: *che spettacolo*! What a show!

Arche Scaligeri

ⓘ *Via Arche Scaligeri, T045-803 2726.*

The 14th-century Gothic iron fence and the raised temples covered with overbearing *baldachini* (canopies) do not provide the most soothing setting for the tombs of Verona's infamous ruling family. But, then again, the Scaligeris were soldiers, murderers and tyrants, so, perhaps, there really is no rest for the wicked. The biggest tomb, a pyramidal affair with a convoluted Gothic pinnacle topped by a horse and rider, is that of Cangrande II. The *baldachino* for Mastino II competes with an even more over-the-top one for Cansignorio,

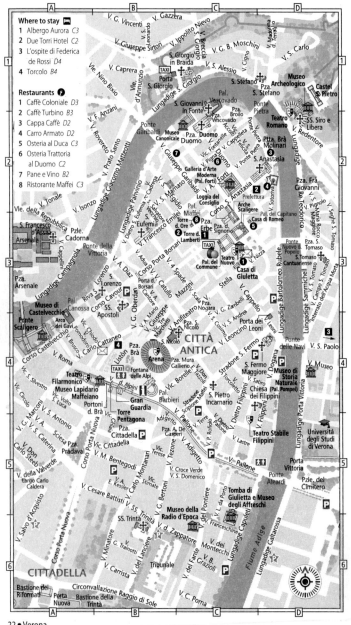

Where to stay 🛏
1 Albergo Aurora *C3*
2 Due Torri Hotel *C2*
3 L'ospite di Federica de Rossi *D4*
4 Torcolo *B4*

Restaurants 🍴
1 Caffè Coloniale *D3*
2 Caffè Turbino *B3*
3 Cappa Caffè *D2*
4 Carro Armato *D2*
5 Osteria al Duca *C3*
6 Osteria Trattoria al Duomo *C2*
7 Pane e Vino *B2*
8 Ristorante Maffei *C3*

CITTÀ ANTICA

CITTADELLA

The Scaligeri

The Scaligeri (or the della Scala family) are the most famous in Veronese history and held the office of *podestà* (mayor) for many generations. Mastino I (the 'mastiff') was the first Scaligeri elected to the position in 1259 and, liking it so much, he passed a law making him *podestà* until his death. He was assassinated by aggrieved *signori* in 1277 and the election of his son, Alberto, to the role instigated 30 years of fighting with the rival San Bonifacio and Este families. Alberto's son, Cangrande I ('big dog' – real name Bartolemeo), inherited the title in 1311 and despite his brutality, left a legacy of grand buildings and artistic treasures. A fierce soldier, autocrat and patron of the arts, he bankrolled Giotto, Dante and Petrarca, as well as significantly expanding Veronese territory. His nephew, Mastino II, took over when he died in 1351 and gained more territory for Verona, before losing much of it to a consortium of families opposed to Scaligeri rule. His son, Cangrande II, took the reins but was deeply disliked – even by his own family – and was eventually murdered by his brother, Cansignorio ('noble dog'), who also dispatched his other brother, Paolo Alboino. Cansignorio left a beautiful legacy of public buildings and statues but his murderous ways turned the Veronese against him and he was forced to flee Verona in 1387. His nephew, Guglielmo, Cangrande II's son, sought to regain the family's reputation but died following a bloody battle to rout the Milanese in 1404, thus ending 145 years of Scaligeri dominance in the city.

The Scaligeri's fondness for canine-related names is unexplained.

while Mastino I's more humble tomb sits against the wall of the church of **Santa Maria Antica**. Rather overshadowed by its surroundings, this modest Romanesque church dates back to the seventh century and was the favoured place of worship for the Scaligeri family, see below. The copy of Cangrande I's equestrian statue (the original is in Castelvecchio) surmounting the doorway suggests it became as much a monument to Scaligeri power as a house of God.

Torre dei Lamberti
ⓘ *Piazza dei Signori, T045-803 2726. Tue-Sun 0930-1930, Mon 1345-1930. To climb: €2.10, €1.50 students; to take the lift: €2.60, €2 students.*
Started in 1172, the building of this 84m high Romanesque tower took nearly 400 years to complete and was not helped by a lightening strike in 1403. If you climb the 368 steps to the top (the lift only takes you so high), you'll feel the tower vibrate as the two bells, Maragona and Rengo, ring out. But what is temporary deafness when you have before you such breathtaking views of this fine city and beyond?

Galleria d'Arte Moderna
ⓘ *Palazzo della Ragione, Piazza dei Signori. Check with tourism.verona.it for details.*
In 2012, this remarkable collection of contemporary art and all future curated exhibitions will move from Palazzo Forti to Palazzo della Ragione. There are curated and touring exhibitions and a collection that includes photography by Cindy Sherman, video installations by Bill Viola and sculpture by Louise Bourgeois.

Centro Internazionale di Fotografia

ⓘ *Cortile del Tribunale, piazza Viviani 5, T045-800 7490. Tue-Sun 1000-1900.*

Located amongst the excavated ruins of long-abandoned Roman sewers, this gallery provides a great setting for some prestigious exhibitions by mainly Italian photographers.

Casa di Giulietta

ⓘ *Via Cappello 23, T045-803 4303. Mon 1330-1930, Tue-Sun 0830-1930, courtyard free, house €6.*

Originally built in the 13th century for the Cappello family, this courtyard palazzo was converted into a museum to Shakespeare's tragic heroine in the mid 1990s, although there is nothing to connect the Cappellos with the fictional Capulets. As you walk along via Cappello you will become aware that there is a bit of a bottleneck ahead: young Veronese hang around smoking, shouting and flirting while groups of elderly tourists stand with puzzled, scrunched-up faces that say, "Is this it?". Well as far as a fictional setting for a fictional character goes, it is. The passageway is covered with graffiti: declarations of love in marker pen and Tippex, layered on so thick that the names and sentiments are barely legible and become one multi-coloured blur. There are clusters of colourful padlocks bearing the names of besotted lovers and, at the other side of the dark alley, the scrawls continue despite dramatic threats of hefty fines by the authorities. For those too scared to face a fine, Post-it notes have been employed and create a fluttering relief.

Visitors expecting a pristine dream scene can barely hide their disappointment at the untidy graphic displays of love and the gangs of raucous young people but there is something truly magical about Juliet's house and balcony. After all, *Romeo and Juliet* is a story of young, all-consuming, destructive love that didn't care about the old folks and their expectations. So, while the tourist attraction itself is a manufactured stage set, the youth of Verona have stuck two fingers up to the authorities and claimed Juliet and her balcony as their own.

Inside the courtyard, all eyes focus on the balcony, although hands veer towards the statue of Juliet cast in bronze at the back wall: rubbing her breast apparently brings luck in love. You can enter the Renaissance-style palazzo to see the bed and some costumes from the 1968 Franco Zefferelli film and an original fresco by Veronese.

Tomba di Giulietta and the Musei degli Affreschi

ⓘ *Via del Pontiere 35, T045-800 0361. Mon 1345-1930, Tue-Sun 0830-1930, €3.*

It's not just the tourist industry that milks Juliet for all she is worth. The Capuchin monastery of San Francesco al Corso is in on the act too, claiming to house Juliet's final resting place. This could so easily have been a cheesy pastiche but in this vaulted room deep in the crypt, with a Gothic window imbuing a golden hue to the crumbling bricks, there is an atmosphere that is quite moving. And, when you realize the sarcophagus is empty, it makes your hair stand on end. If you are too embarrassed to admit to visiting the tomb of a non-existent woman, there is the thin excuse of the fresco museum upstairs.

Castelvecchio and Museo Civico d'Arte

ⓘ *Corso Castelvecchio 2, T045-806 2611. Mon 1330-1930, Tue-Sun 0830-1930, €8, €3 under 14s.*

Built by Cangrande II in 1357 as a discreet little pied-à-terre, the castle consists of two huge blocks that sit on either side of the ponte Scaligero: one served as a military base and stores; the other as the ruler's residence. Following the fall of the Scaligeri, the castle was occupied in turn by the ruling Visconti family, officials from the Venetian Republic and then Napoleon's men.

The castle now holds the civic art museum. Downstairs a collection of carvings and statues from the Middle Ages is displayed in a serene exhibition space by Carlo Scarpa (1906-1978), the Venetian architect whose modernist vision was informed and resourced by materials popular in the past. Light flows in through the windows caressing the somewhat clumsy sculptures of Jesus and the Saints and casting a hazy light that assists the spiritual context. Upstairs there are paintings and decorative arts by Tintoretto, Tiepolo, Veronese, Bellini and Pisanello. It is also worth strolling around Scarpa's gardens in the courtyard, which mix greenery with old (the statue of Cangrande) and new (a tufa waterpool) features. It has a few welcome places to sit down for some sensory respite.

The red-brick crenellated **ponte Scaligero** links the castle with the Arsenale across the Adige. It was bombed by the Americans during World War II but rebuilt soon after using the remains that they dug out of the river. There are walkways along the battlements and a number of observation points which provide great photo opportunities.

Basilica San Zeno Maggiore

ⓘ *Piazza San Zeno, T045-592813. Mar-Oct daily 0830-1800, Nov-Feb Tue-Sat 1000-1600, Sun 1300-1700, €2.50. Visitors discouraged during Mass.*

This 12th-century basilica is dedicated to Verona's patron saint, San Zeno (died AD 380), who was the city's eighth bishop and also the patron saint of fishermen. Made of local rose brick and creamy toned tufa, it glows in the late afternoon sun. The 62-m campanile and the nave with its ship's keel ceiling and Gothic adornment were added in the late 1300s. Two marble lions support the columns of the porch which is intricately carved with scenes from Genesis by Nicolò, dating from 1135. Within the bronze panels of the wooden doors and the bas relief above there are simple, almost comic, images from the life of San Zeno. Inside, Lorenzo Veneziano's *Crucifixion* (1360) hangs on the west wall. You won't be the only one to admire Andrea Mantegna's altarpiece *Madonna and Child Enthroned with Saints* (1457-59): Napoleon pilfered it for his collection in Paris. The Romanesque cloister with Gothic arches may be a mish-mash of styles but it is undoubtedly tranquil.

Museo della Radio Epoca

ⓘ *ITIS Galileo Ferraris, via del Pontiere 40, T045-505855, museodellaradio.com. Mon-Fri 0900-1800, €5.*

Not far from the Tomba di Giulietta is this wonderful collection of radios, from art deco to swingable handheld sets. This museum documents their development with nerdy but sincere enthusiasm. (For those who are wondering, Galileo Ferraris was the physicist who discovered alternating currents.)

Duomo

ⓘ *Piazza Duomo, T045-592 813. Mon-Sat 0930-1800, Sun 1300-1800, €2.50. Strictly no bare legs or shoulders.*

As grand as some of the Venetian churches, Verona's cathedral took 500 years to complete and is full of splendid craftsmanship. The architect Sansovino designed the choir and the Cappella Nichesola, which houses Titian's vibrant *Assumption* (1540). Through an old door in the far wall you can access **San Giovanni in Fonte**. This carefully renovated Romanesque church would seem austere were it not for the rich tones of its marble. Its huge baptismal font (1200) is made from a single block, carved with scenes from the Gospel (some of them gruesome). Next to it is the church of **Sant'Elena**, built in the ninth century. Excavations under glass show the mosaics and stones of an even earlier Christian church, dating from AD 362.

From the piazza in front of the Duomo you can visit the cloisters, a beautiful arched courtyard now home to private residents. Also on piazza Duomo is the **Biblioteca Capitulare**, which houses artworks and hundreds of rare liturgical and jurisprudential texts, and the **Museo Canonicale** ① *Fri 1000-1230, Sat 1000-1300 and 1430-1800, Sun 1430-1800, €2.50*, a much celebrated collection of paintings and statues of the saints and the Madonna dating from the 12th to the 18th centuries.

Sant'Anastasia
① *Piazza Sant'Anastasia, T045-592813. Mon-Sat 0930-1800, Sun 1300-1800, €2.50.*
This big Gothic bruiser of a church is softened by an enchanting fresco by Antonio di Pisanello and by the two marble hunchbacks – one stooped, one sitting – that support the water fonts. These were carved by Paolo Veronese's father in 1495.

San Fermo Maggiore
① *Stradone San Fermo, T045-800 7287. Mon-Sat 0930-1800, Sun 1300-1800, €2.50.*
The layers of Verona's history are laid bare in the structure of this fascinating church. The original fifth-century church housed the relics of the saints Fermo and Rustico. A few walls remain but it was largely replaced in the 11th century by a Romanesque church (now accessed from the cloisters). In the 13th century, a Gothic church was built on top; this is the big gingerbread edifice you see today.

Santa Maria in Organo
① *Via Santa Maria in Organo. Mon-Sat 0930-1800, Sun 1300-1800, €2.50.*
You'll find this little church next to the Giardino Giusti. It has a wooden choir lovingly carved by Giovanni da Verona (1457-1525), a monk whose talent for intarsia and marquetry is without parallel.

Teatro Romano and Museo Archeologico
① *Rigaste Redentore 2, T045-800 0360. Mon 1330-1930, Tue-Sun 0830-1930 (ticket office closes at 1845), €3. For information about performances and the Shakespeare festival in July: T045-807 7201, estateteatraleveronese.it.*
Climb all the steps to the top of the hill and you'll realise how perfectly located this Roman theatre is. But it's not until you see Palladio's model of it in the archaeological museum that you can appreciate just how breathtakingly beautiful it must have been.

Like the Arena, the Teatro Romano suffered the effects of an earthquake and has lost some of its stones to other buildings in the city but there is still enough here to stage an awesome performance. What remains are the *scena* (stage) and the semicircular *cavea* (auditorium) as well as some deep steps which still serve as seating. The back wall of the stage (*scaenae frons*) has been rebuilt. Roman plays tended to copy the Greek style but were certainly bawdier with more rough and tumble.

Head up the steps to the archaeological museum, housed in the former convent of San Girolamo. There are some small rooms showing Estruscan and Roman figurines, ceramics and tools from digs around the city. However, it is the views out of the tiny windows that will catch your eye. The larger rooms have Roman busts without noses, headless sculptures, some interesting mosaics as well as Palladio's model of the theatre. The high point is the walk through the former residential wing into the gardens, where tombstones, capitals, columns and even an old chariot are displayed. Sitting amongst these ruins, looking out over the remarkable panorama is a generous reward for the toil up the hill.

Giardino Giusti
ⓘ *Via Giardino Giusti 2, T045-803 4029. Apr-Sep 0900-2000, Oct-Mar 0900-1900, €5.*
The Palazzo Giusti is located in a residential area, just along from the Teatro Romano, and gives no hint of the treat that lies behind its walls. Beyond the courtyard is a Renaissance garden whose timeless beauty has inspired poets, including Goethe on a visit in 1786. You can read his musings on one of the first trees you see as you enter. Laid out in 1580 by Agostino Giusti, the gardens follow a simple symmetry, structured by cypresses, box hedges and gravel paths that lead up to a stone-terraced wood. The palazzo blocks any views of the city but the sense of enclosure is welcome in such a dreamy setting.

Museo Civico di Storia Naturale
ⓘ *Lungadige Porta Vittoria 9, T045-807 9400, museostorianaturaleverona.it.Mon-Thu and Sat 0900-1900, Sun 1400-1900, €3.*
If it's raining, this museum of botanic, zoological and geological objects will help while away a couple of hours. It is an archetypal civic museum and has a dusty, dated feel but don't let first impressions put you off. There are some huge fossils of weird prehistoric fish, the bones of a species of brown bear that once roamed the wilds of the northern Veneto, an abundance of taxidermy and a display of limestone and marble which may inspire you to do up the bathroom when you get home.

A walk through Central Verona

Begin at **piazza Bra**, where you can admire the Roman Arena while sipping a coffee in one of the many bars that make up the Listone. The balcony at No. 18 is famous as the venue for Garibaldi's 'Rome or death' speech in 1867. To the hard right is a double-arched gate, the portoni Bra, which leads to Porta Nuova train station and the city walls.

Walk along the arcaded 17th-century Gran Guardia, which was built by Domenico Curtoni (c1610), and part of an interior city wall. These fortifications were the work of the della Scala or Scaligeri family, who ruled Verona in the 13th century and needed to keep their numerous enemies out of the city. Walking round the piazza, on your right you'll see the flashy neoclassical Palazzo Barbieri (1848), which is now the city hall, while across from the Arena are pleasant cedar- and pine-filled gardens. Walk through these to see a statue of Victor Emanuel II, first king of the united Italy.

To your left is the Arena and, ahead, the Louis Vuitton shop which marks the start of via Mazzini. This glamorous thoroughfare leads towards **piazza Erbe**, which was built on the site of the former Roman forum. A **market** ⓘ *Mon-Sat 0800-1900*, is still held here but it has dwindled in size and quality: if you're looking for a Romeo and Juliet snowstorm to take home, here's where to find it. Standing at the **Fontana Madonna Verona** (1368), which was constructed out of a font from Sant'Anastasia, you'll see the column of San Marco that denotes the presence of the Venetians, who added Verona to their territory in 1405. Napoleon's men pulled it down when Venice fell in 1797 but it was re-erected in 1886. Behind the column is the huge baroque **Palazzo Maffei**, which stands on the site of the old Roman Capitol. It is crowned with statues of Hercules, Jupiter, Venus, Mercury, Apollo and

Minerva. If you dine in the wonderful Maffei (see page 29), be charming to the waiter and he may just take you downstairs to see the ruins. To the left of Palazzo Maffei is **Torre del Gardelo**, built in 1370. Its bell is now at Castelvecchio. Shops line the western side of the piazza with a small *piazzetta* housing the Romanesque **Domus Mercatorum** (1301) or Merchants' House. Near the Fontana you will also see the **Berlina**, a canopied construction from the 12th century where ceremonies involving the *podestà* or mayor were held.

Now walk along via della Costa and through the **Arco della Costa** (arch of the rib) – so called because a whale bone dangles inexplicably from it – to the grander **piazza dei Signori**. Immediately to the right, at 83 m high, is the **Torre dei Lamberti**, which affords the best views of Verona. It was built in the 12th century, although the belfry wasn't added until 1464. Further on and into piazza dei Signori there are three arches to your right. The first small arch leads to cortile Mercato Vecchio, a pink and white brick courtyard where **Palazzo del Comune** (also called Palazzo della Ragione, the Palace of Reason, built in 1193) sits at the top of a magnificent Renaissance staircase, the **Scala della Ragione**.

The second larger arch leads to via Dante where there are some exposed Roman excavations. The third and final arch leads to cortile del Tribune and the **Scavi Scaligeri** (the Roman excavations which you can see in the cortile under glass) and the **Centro Internazionale di Fotografia** in Palazzo Viviani (see page 24).

Looking across the piazza and straight at the statue of Dante, the building to your left (near the entrance to Piazza Erbe) is the 17th-century Venetian-style **Domus Nova** and the Renaissance **Loggia del Consiglio** (1492), the meeting room for government. The building is crowned with five statues: Vitruvius, local Roman poet Catallus, Pliny the Elder, Emilio Marco and Cornelius Nepos. Straight ahead is the Renaissance loggia by Fra' Giocondo (1493) which was home to the Council during Venetian rule.

The statue of Dante recognizes Verona's love of the great medieval humanist who visited his chums, the Scaligeris, in 1306, and then again in 1314. He may have loved Verona enough to have returned but the city's beauty did not still his raging heart. The poet, having fallen foul of the Florentine ruling elite, had been exiled from his beloved Florence, stripped of his property and left impoverished and destitute. Sorely aggrieved at the time, he developed deep grudges against those who crossed him and took his revenge by trapping them for eternity (at least literary eternity) in the rings of hell in his *Inferno*. Pause for a coffee or a Spritz close to his statue by Ugo Zannoni (1865) and be grateful you never fell foul of the man.

Verona listings

For hotel and restaurant price codes and other relevant information, see pages 11-14.

◉ Where to stay

Verona *p21, map p22*
€€€ Due Torri Hotel, *Piazza Sant'Anastasia 4, T045-595044, duetorrihotels.com*. If you want to luxe it up in Verona, this is where to do it. It's just around the corner from some of the best bars in the city and right next to the church, so both sins and redemption are well catered for. The bedrooms are plush and the sparkling marble bathrooms are perfect places to pamper yourself. Lounge around in the lavish public rooms, if you're not put off by the staff's air of cool hauteur.
€€ Albergo Aurora, *Piazza Erbe, T045-594717, hotelaurora.biz*. In a great location right on piazza Erbe, this hotel has a typical Italian reception area, with efficient female staff doing all the work while the men seem to just sit around reading newspapers. Its

19 rooms are plain but have everything you need (including air-conditioning units). However it's the fabulous roof terrace overlooking the piazza that is the selling point. This is where breakfast is served.

€€ Ca' dell'Orto, *Via Francesco da Levanto, T045- 830 3554, cadellorto.it. Bus 61/62.* Only 2 km (a 25-min walk or a €15 taxi ride) from the city centre, following the bend of the river Adige, this 'aparthotel' has nicely furnished and fully equipped rooms (those on the top floor have huge skylights) and well-kept grounds with a pool. Breakfasts are bountiful.

€€ Hotel Torcolo, *Vicolo Listone 3, T045- 800 7512, hoteltorcolo.it. Closed Feb.* Just off piazza Bra, this hotel is run with old-fashioned hospitality by two thoroughly modern ladies. Popular with opera goers, it appeals to those who appreciate a bit of care and attention. The rooms are nothing fancy but still good quality and the bathrooms are spick and span. Breakfasts are extra (€8-13) and are served in the courtyard but, if you're ravenous, you will get more for €13 from one of the cafés nearby.

€ B&B In The Sun, *Via San Vincenzo 3A, T045-551786, bbinthesun.com. Bus 51.* Located 6 km north of the city centre on the vineyard-swathed Torricelle hills, this large farmhouse has been converted with style and enthusiasm. The rooms are simple and contemporary with firm beds and down-filled pillows, and the rural location ensures a good night's rest, uninterrupted by the Vespas that punctuate sleep in the city. Breakfast is all organic and if you want to cook your own dinner you can use the kitchen. There are even laundry facilities. A taxi to here costs €15-20.

Self-catering

L'ospite di Federica de Rossi, *Via XX Settembre 3, T045-803 6994, lospite.com. €35-180 (depending on size of room and time of year).* We're not surprised that Ms de Rossi is proud to put her name to this establishment. Its six simply furnished apartments are of varying sizes so can accommodate singles, couples and even small families. All are spotless and kitted out with everything you need. This is an excellent base for a holiday in the Veneto. Federica or Flavio are always on hand to offer advice and will go the extra mile to make sure you have everything you need.

🍴 Restaurants

Verona *p21, map p22*

€€€ Enoteca Segreta, *Vicolo Samaritana 10, T045-801 5824, enotecasegreta.it. Mon-Sat 1900-0200.* As well as being an excellent restaurant, this enoteca is a great place for wine tasting and aperitivi. The owner is a sommelier and for the tasting he serves wines combined with a different cheese or salume from Verona. He tells you the history of the wine and the vineyard it comes from.

€€€ Ristorante Maffei, *Piazza Erbe 38, T045-801 0015, ristorantemaffei.it. Daily 1200-1400 and 1900-2200.* This is where the locals go for a special night out. The Maffei kitchen experiments with new colours and textures to add something extra to classic dishes. Their risotto with melon puree or bigoli cooked in Amarone are so good, you'll find yourself writing about them on postcards home. There's seating both inside and in the courtyard recessed from the piazza and some beautifully lit Roman ruins downstairs.

€€ Carro Armato, *Vicolo Gatto 2a, T045-803 0175. Mon, Tue amd Thu-Sat 1000-0200, Sun 1000-2400.* This is an excellent spot for some informal dining with, perhaps, a greater emphasis on drinking. The heavy wooden benches and sturdy tables make you feel as though you could easily take on the wine list and menu but beware: portions are generous. Everything has a made-by-mamma feel about it. Simple dishes, such as *gnocchi di patate* served with a sweet tomato sauce and a dollop of ricotta, earn cries of '*buonissimi!*'

€€ **Osteria al Duca**, *Via Arche Scaligeri 2, T045-594474. May-Oct Mon-Fri 1200-1430 and 1800-2230, Nov-Apr Mon and Wed-Sat 1200-1430 and 1830-2230*. Book in advance as this place is popular with returning American tourists who are chummy with the owners, the Montecchi family. You will eat a fine meal here from the meat- and fish-orientated menu: *bigoli con le sarde* (bigoli pasta with sardines) or *agnello arrosto* (roast lamb) with fragrant fried potatoes are typical. An ample two-course lunch costs just €13: a bargain considering the quality. Puddings are also good, especially the *biscotti* dipped in *vin santo*.

€€ **Osteria Trattoria al Duomo**, *Via Duomo 7a, T045-800 4505. Mon-Sat 1100-1430 and 1800-2230*. This wonderful tavern feels and sounds like it's the spiritual home for rock children of the 1960s and '70s. The wine list is long (and cheap) and the food is splendid: nothing particularly fancy, just substantial, wholesome dishes like *bigoli con ragu d'asino* (bigoli pasta with donkey sauce) and cherry tomato-tossed spaghetti with the perkiest rocket. The tiramisu is great, but copious use of fruit sauces renders many puddings a let-down.

€ **Pane e Vino**, *Via Garibaldi 16a, T045-800 8261. Wed-Mon 1100-1500 and 1800-2300*. Just down the road from the Scaligeri tombs, this popular trattoria offers a €10 lunch that includes starter, main course and half a carafe of wine and water. The food is so good and the service is so forthcoming that you keep wonering what the catch is. There isn't one. It's all hearty stuff: risotto, beef cooked in Amarone and *bollito con la peará* (boiled meat served with bread sauce). Doesn't sound much, but it's delicious.

Cafés and bars

Bar al Ponte, *Via Ponte Pietra 26, T045-927 5032. Tue-Sun 1200-2400*. Walking down from ponte Pietra, if you blink you might miss this bar because it is below street level. It has a little terrace on the river offering a breathtaking view and a gentle breeze. It's particularly lovely by candlelight.

Caffè Coloniale, *Piazzetta Viviani 14c, T337-472737. Tue-Sat 0745-2400, Sun 0945-2400*. Located between piazza Erbe and Casa di Giulietta, this is run by real coffee enthusiasts. You can opt for a fancy, cream-laden Viennese version or a heady Moroccan blend. There are seats inside and out.

Caffè Turbino, *Corso di Porta Borsari 15d, T045-803 1313. Mon-Sat 0715-2100*. A very small café with a very large chandelier and an even larger reputation. It's been packing them in for years. If you like the coffee, you can buy some to take home.

Cantina del Bugiardo, *Corso Portoni Borsari 17, T045-591869. Tue-Sun 1100-2200*. This cantina is very popular for its *bocconcini* (bread topped with all kind of delicacies) and other snacks to eat with a good glass of wine.

Cappa Café, *Piazzetta Bra Molinari 1, T045-800 4549. Daily 0730-0200*. This rather boho spot does a lovely cappuccino and has a terrace round the back that looks out over the Adige towards San Pietro.

Gelato Ponte Pietra, *Via Ponte Pietra 23. Mon 1530-2000, Tue-Sun 1100-2200*. The local's favourite gelateria: home-made flavours sold on a little street behind the Duomo.

L'Aquila Nera Caffè, *Via Pellicciai 2, T045-801 0172, aquilaneraverona.com. Daily 1700-2300*. A very elegant café where you can sit down in a comfortable armchair and relax. Great choice of wine, champagne, plus a rich buffet.

M27, *Via G Mazzini 27/a, T045-803 4242. Tue-Sun 0800-0200*. Great list of snacks, aperitivi and drinks, plus the best freshly prepared sandwiches in town. Open late.

Osteria Monte Baldo, *Via Rosa 12, T045-803 0579. Mon-Sat 1000-1500 and 1700-2100*. This is one of the oldest osterie in Verona. It offers *tartine* (canapés) and wine, oysters on Friday and Saturday, and it's open for lunch during the week.

Osteria Sottoriva, *Via Sottoriva 9a, T045-801 4323. Thu-Tue 1100-2230.* Want to know what the best wines of the Veneto are? Try them here, in this convivial bar.

Savoia, *Via Roma 1b, piazza Bra, T045-800 2211. Tue-Sun 1100-2200.* A top-quality range of artisan ice creams are on offer here. Try a slider (ice cream sandwiched between wafers) or the Gianduiotto, served in a cup: it's a chocolate-lover's dream.

♪ Entertainment

Verona *p21, map p22*
Cinema
Teatro Stimate, *Piazza Cittadella, via Montarino 1, T045-800 0878.* Shows art house and independent films with, joy of joys, subtitles rather than dodgy dubbing. English-language films on Tuesdays.

Clubs
Alter Ego Club, *Via Torricelle 9, T045-915130, alteregoclub.it. Jun-Sep Fri-Sat 2230-0300 (sometimes 0600).* House, prog and euro pop are served up to a molto-trendy crowd at this bizarre club in the hills. A taxi will cost around €22 from the centre of Verona. Check the website for details.

Gay and lesbian
Caffè Bukowski, *Via Amanti 6. Wed-Mon 1900-0200.* This rather avant-garde disco has happy hours in the early evening but doesn't really get going until 2200. The music is a mix of everything from Hi-NRG to Elvis to, er, Dido.

Romeos Club, *Via Giolfino 12, Zona Porta Vescovo, T045-840 3215, romeosclubverona. blogspot.com. Tue-Sat 2300-0530.* There are thumping euro beats at this shirts-off gay club. It also hosts occasional film nights.

Music and theatre
Tickets for the Verona Jazz Festival (June), the Shakespeare Festival (June to August) and the Dance Festival (August), as well as tickets for visiting artists and shows, are available from **Assessorato alla Cultura di Verona** (Palazzo Barbieri, angolo Via Leoncino 61, T045-806 6485, estateteatrale veronese.it, box office Mon-Sat 1030-1300 and 1600-1900 and on day of performance). As well as the venues listed here, festival events are held in the Teatro Romano, Corte Mercato Vecchio and Giardino Giusti.

Arena, *Piazza Bra, T045-800 3204, arena. it.* This is the ultimate venue for opera in the summer, plus occasional gigs by big international rock and pop acts visiting Verona. The opera season starts in June and runs until August with four or five different operas on different nights. Tickets start at €17 for the marble stairs at the back and go up to €139 for the plush red seats at the front. Performances start at 2100 and can last until midnight.

Interzona, *Via Scuderlando 4, T045-201 1005, izona.it.* This edgy venue hosts a diverse programme of rock, punk, folk, jazz and video art performances in a disused industrial unit in the south of the city. Check the website for details. You'll need a taxi to get there and back.

Teatro Filarmonico, *Via dei Mutilati 4, T045-805 1891, arena.it. Box office: Via Roma 3, T045-800 5151. Daily 1000-1200 and 1630-1930 or until 2100 on the day of performance.* Bombed by the Americans during the war, this grand venue has finally been restored to its former glory and hosts classical concerts, ballets and opera during the winter season.

◎ Shopping

Verona *p21, map p22*
Most shops are open from 0930 to 1300, when they close for a long lunch and siesta, before opening again from 1600 to 1900. Most are closed on a Sunday and some are also closed on a Monday morning. There are sales in Verona in January and February and from late July to early August.

Art and antiques

There is an outdoor antiques market at Piazza San Zeno on the third Saturday of every month. In addition to the ones listed here, you'll find a number of antique shops on and around corso Sant' Anastasia.

Antichità Due Torri, *Corso Santa' Anastasia 29, T045 800 2414.* Marvellous old prints and paintings as well as objects of beauty.

Antichità Smeraldo, *Vicolo Due Stelle 5. T045-801 0667.* Antique demi-johns, chandeliers and porcelain are just some of the things you'll find in this cornucopia.

Books

Bazzani Stampe Antiche – Libreria Antiquaria, *Via Stella 20, T045-597621, libreriabazzanistampeantiche.com.* Behind a 16th-century arch, this roomy shop sells beautiful old books and maps.

FNAC, *Via Cappello 34, T045-806 3811.* This French-owned megastore sells music and electronics, as well as books, and has a café with internet access.

Ghelfi & Barbato, *Via Mazzini 21, T045-800 2306.* On the main drag, this is the place to find a large selection of maps and travel guides in English, as well as cookbooks.

Liberia Novecento, *Via Santa Maria in Chiavica 3.* A mix of early 20th century English and Italian travel guides, art books, prints, political manifestos and some curious tomes that defy categorization.

Clothing

There's some excellent clothes shopping to be done in Verona. The main streets to explore are via Mazzini (for Gucci, Diesel, Furla, Mandarina Duck), via Cappello (for more designer names, like Armani) and corso Porta Borsari (for shoes) but the web of little streets that run off these thoroughfares have some great little independent boutiques too.

Baol, *Vicolo Stella 9, T045-800 4973.* You may not recognise the names on the labels but they are worn by the less bling, most independently minded Veronese ladies.

Cecile, *Via Salvatore, corte Reggia 9, T045-803 6247.* Vintage and second-hand shops are not exactly ten-a-penny in Italy but this is a treasure trove with Prada and even some Pucci calling your name.

Opticus, *Via Roma 5, T045-594804, opticusverona.it.* Eccentric and customized spectacles and sunglasses in every colour.

Department stores

Coin, *Via Cappello 30, T045-803 4321.* Great for good quality fashion, underwear, homewares and accessories. The cosmetic department is pretty good too.

Upim, *Via Mazzini 6, T045-596701.* Lots of run-of-the-mill items but the kitchen section is particularly good.

Food and drink

Calimala Chocolat, *Vicolo Crocini 4a, T045-800 5478.* Hand-made chocolates and sweet treats.

PAM, *Via dei Mulati 3, T045-803 2822.* This supermarket is full of fresh local produce and every basic ingredient, as well as coffee, pasta and alcohol at knock-down prices.

Pasticceria Flego, *Via Stella 13, T045-803 2471.* Take home some mini artisan pastries that ooze with almond cream, spiced apple, praline or chocolate.

Salumeria Albertini, *Corso Sant' Anastasia, T045-803 1074.* Whether you are taking home a *panettone* or a piece of *baccalà* (dried cod) for gran or just fancy a few slices of *sopressa* (sausage) and some bread, Albertini's is pricey but good.

Souvenirs

The market in piazza Erbe (Mon-Sat 0800-1900) sells cheesy Romeo and Juliet snowstorms and Arena di Verona ashtrays.

ⓐ What to do

Verona *p21, map p22*
Cultural
If you want to learn the language, Verona is one of the best cities to take a course.

Lingua IT, *Via Francesco Emilei 24, T045-597975, linguait.it. €610 for a 4-week, 80-hour course and €390 for a 2-week, 40-hour course.* Just off Piazza Erbe, this young, on-the-ball language school delivers well-structured intensive courses that provide great value for money and a fighting chance of understanding and being understood in Italian.

Football

Verona has two teams that share the **Stadio Marc'Antonio Bentegodi** at piazzale Olimpia. **AC Chievo Verona** (Via Galvani 3, T045-575779, chievoverona. it) are known as the '*mussi volanti*' or flying donkeys and are in Serie A. **Hellas Verona FC** (Verona Point, via Cristoforo 30, T045-575005, hellasverona.it), nicknamed the 'Mastiffs', have an old-school following that has stuck with them despite a fall in fortunes: they now play in the Lega Pro Prima Divisione, equivalent to the English First Division. Check out their websites for dates of home games or the daily *Corriere dello Sport* or L'Arena newspapers.

Food and wine

The Provincia di Verona tourist information website (tourism.verona.it) has information about local *cantine* that welcome visitors and a route map in the 'Enjoying our Land' section. The Verona area is particularly famous for its Valpolicella and Soave. Italy's most important wine trade fair, **Vinitaly** (vinitaly.com) is held in Verona over five days in April. Although this is primarily for wine trade professionals, there are events around town, such as 'Vinitaly for you' in Gran Guardia, that are aimed at those who simply enjoy wine.

Veneto Tours, *theothersideofvenice.com.* The Valpolicella wine tour whirls you up and over the undulating hills around Verona in a Mercedes and introduces you to *cantine* where you'll learn the craft behind Amarone, Ricotto and Ripasso. Expect to taste the best (and a fair bit

of it). They also offer a Soave wine tour. From €120pp.

Wellbeing

Villa dei Cedri, *Piazza di Sopra 4, Colà di Lazise, T045-759 0988, villadeicedri.com. Mon-Thu 0900-2100, Fri-Sat 0900-0200, Sun and public hols 0900-2300, €16-21.* Just 25 km from Verona, this spa beside a lake with hot thermal waters is open all year round. It's lit up at night creating a magical, steaming environment for pure relaxation.

⊖ Transport

Verona *p21, map p22*
The centre of Verona is compact enough to explore happily on foot. There are orange **AMT** buses for travel around the city and blue **APTV** buses for transport to outlying destinations. The **Verona Card** (€8 for one day; €12 for three days) admits you to a number of Verona's sights and allows free travel on AMT buses. It can be bought in shops, museums, monuments and tobacconists (look for the T sign). Tourists can hire bikes for free from the tourist information office at Porta Nuova train station by leaving an identity card or passport. **Radio Taxi**, T045-532666.

Bus

The bus station, **Autostazione di Verona Porta Nuova**, is on piazzale XXV Aprile, T045-887 1111 (AMT), T045-805 7811 (APTV), amt.it, apt.vr.it. There are frequent buses to Venice (2 hrs), Vicenza (45 mins) and Padua (1 hr).

Train

The train station, **Porta Nuova FS**, is on piazzale XXV Aprile, T045-800 0861, trenitalia.it. There are hourly train services to Milan (2 hrs), Venice (1½ hrs), Vicenza (30 mins) and Padua (45 mins).

❶ Directory

Verona *p21, map p22*
Money ATMs at the train station; via Mazzini; piazza Erbe. **Medical services Ospedale Civile Maggiore Borgo Trento**, piazzale Stefani 1, T045-812 1111. Call T1100 for the three nearest open pharmacies. **Post office** Piazza Isolo 13, T045-805 0311 (Mon-Sat 0830-1830). **Tourist information** IAT, via degli Alpini 9, T045-806 8680, tourism.verona.it (Mon-Sat 0900-1900, Sun 0900-1500); **IAT**, Porta Nuova FS, T045-800 0861 (Mon-Sat 0900-1800, Sun 0900-1500). This is temporarily closed whilst the station gets a refurb.

Contents

Vicenza & around

Vicenza is one of Italy's most beautiful cities but it is not one of its best known. The Romans snatched it from the Gauls in AD 49 but after the fall of the empire it changed hands many times and was always a poor relation to Verona until the Venetians took charge in 1404. The 1500s saw the emergence of this remarkable city, thanks to the extraordinary talent and commitment of Andrea Palladio. The Renaissance's rediscovery of classicism, the liberal arts and the humanities created a fertile ground for the ideas of the architect who, reintroduced the columns, domes and porticos of classical architecture to transform the city and architecture itself. Not *everything* in Vicenza was designed or built by Palladio but there can be few other cities where the work of a single architect can be seen round every corner.

With its famous gold fairs (in January, May, September), Vicenza today is the third most productive city in Italy; not bad for a place that has only 120,000 inhabitants. So, it's well off, friendly and stunning, particularly first thing in the morning. Is it the perfect city? Not quite. The US army base, located outside the city and controversially expanded in 2009, is a noticeable presence: take an early morning stroll around Vicenza and you'll see the streets become a training ground for huffing, sweating troops.

To the south of Vicenza lie the Berici hills, while, to the north, in the foothills of the Sette Comuni, are the splendid medieval towns of Thiene, Marostica and Bassano del Grappa.

Vicenza

Piazza dei Signori

Piazza dei Signori is situated on what is believed to have been the original Roman Forum and is linked to piazza delle Biade to the east, piazza delle Erbe to the south and piazzetta Palladio to the west. The border with piazza delle Biade is marked by two columns which were constructed to remind the Vicentini who were in charge: the Venetian lion of St Mark (1464) spreads its wings atop one, while Christ (1649) looks down from the other.

Dominating the piazza is the **Basilica Palladiana** (or Palazzo della Ragione). Palladio liked to bring sacred design into secular use, so, although it's called a Basilica, this is a judicial rather than religious building. The Gothic hall with its large ship's keel roof was built in the mid 15th century by Domenico da Venezia. Palladio won the commission to refurbish it in 1549, while he was still relatively inexperienced. His idea was to sheathe the building in a two-storey loggia, with Doric columns on the ground floor and Ionic columns on the upper. Entablatures topped both rows of columns and were crowned with a balustrade populated by 23 deeply flattering statues of the Albanese family. Palladio had been dead for 34 years before the final Ionic row was finished in 1614.

Across the piazza, the grandiose **Loggia del Capitaniato** (also known as Loggia Bernarda) was the former headquarters of the city's Venetian rulers and is now home to the city council. Palladio was commissioned to design it in 1571 to mark the Republic's victory in the Battle of Lepanto and he sought to match the Basilica in size and majesty. However, the project ran out of steam, leaving the loggia with three bays rather than the intended seven and making it look slightly misshapen. Nevertheless, it is far more imposing than most town halls.

The **Torre di Piazza** (or Torre di Bissari) was begun in the 12th century and added to once in 1311, then, again, in the 15th century until it reached its full height of 82 m. It's a slender thing, with a base that is just 7 m wide. Next to it is the **Palazzo del Podestà**. Built in the 12th century by the Bissari family, it was bought by the authorities in the 13th century and given numerous makeovers.

Piazza delle Erbe, behind the Basilica, also has a tower known as the **Torre del Tormento**. This former prison and torture chamber was a place of dread in medieval times. The piazza also hosts the town's market and has a few interesting bars and restaurants.

Teatro Olimpico

ⓘ *Piazza Matteotti 11, T0444-222800, teatrolimpicovicenza.it. Jul-Aug Tue-Sun 0900-1900, Sep-Jun 0900-1700, single ticket €6 or €8.50 for admission to Museo Civico Pinacoteca and Museo Naturalistico Archeologico, valid for 3 days.*

In 1555 Palladio founded the Accademia Olympica, a culturally enriching club for the great and the good of Vicenza, and used this to build enthusiasm for the creation of an indoor theatre in the Roman style. There's not much to see on the outside except for an iron gate, some architectural remnants and lush ivy caressing the courtyard walls, but Palladio's and Scamozzi's genius was unleashed on the interior.

Palladio's trademark obsessions – proportion, perspective and symmetry – all come together in a remarkably innovative way, creating the illusion that the stage recedes further than it does. The stage forms a rectangle, while the auditorium is a semi-circle with wooden bench seating on a fairly steep rake. A second tier is created by a wooden colonnade with plaster cornicing and detailed figures. The ceiling was later painted to resemble a celestial sky with flitting clouds.

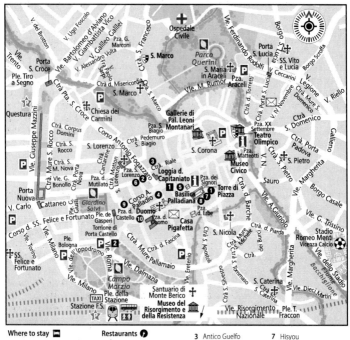

Where to stay 🛏

1 Albergo due Mori
2 Campo Marzio

Restaurants 🍴

1 Amici Miei Restaurant
  and Drinks
2 Antica Casa della Malvasia

3 Antico Guelfo
4 Art Café
5 Caffè Natura
6 Gran Caffè Garibaldi

7 Hisyou
8 Il Grottino
9 Pasticceria Sorarù
10 Righetti

After Palladio's death in 1580, his son Silla oversaw the completion of the auditorium, while Scamozzi got to work on the stage. The permanent stage set looks like stone but is in fact finely carved in wood. It is angled, with a mid-stage opening that, by clever use of foreshortening, depicts the streets of Thebes. Goethe called it "indescribably beautiful" during his 1786 Grand Tour.

The Teatro Olimpico is both the first and last of its kind: the first modern theatre and the only surviving Renaissance theatre. Its first performance was *Oedipus Rex* in 1585. In the late 16th century, the killjoys of the counter-Reformation closed the theatre but, after the Second World War the Academy regrouped and reopened Vicenza's theatrical treasure trove. It now hosts regular summer seasons of music and drama (see page 48).

Museo Civico Pinacoteca

ⓘ *Palazzo Chiericati, piazza Matteotti, T0444-321348, museicivicivicenza.it. Sep-Jun Tue-Sun 0900-1300, Jul-Aug Tue-Sun 1000-1300 , €6.50 or €8.50 for Teatro Olimpico and Museo Naturalistico Archeologico, valid for 3 days.*

Palazzo Chiericati was designed by the city architect in 1550-57. With its unusual layout, open loggias on both the ground floor and *piano nobile*, and elevated, stand-alone position, it is an intriguing building. It makes more sense, however, when you consider that this was once the port area (formerly known as piazza dell'Isola) and the palazzo was designed to sit on the edge of the water.

On the ground floor, the Neri Pozza bequest has three rooms of 19th- and 20th-century Italian artists, while on the second floor, the Pinacoteca is a series of eight understated rooms that are home to Vicenza's huge and impressive civic art collection. Arranged chronologically, you can see the developing techniques, styles and themes used during the Renaissance and Baroque periods. Worth looking out for are Hans Memling's *Calvary* (c1470), Tintoretto's soaring *St Augustine Healing the Lame* (1550), Anthony Van Dyck's *The Three Ages of Man* (1625) and Giovanni Battista Piazzetta's *Ecstasy of St Francis* (1732).

Chiesa di Santa Corona

ⓘ *Contrà Santa Corona 2. Daily 0830-1200 and 1430-1800.*
Built to house a fragment of Jesus' crown of thorns, this Romanesque church has an unfathomable construction which makes it difficult to get your bearings once you are inside. At the fifth altar is Giovanni Bellini's *Baptism of Christ* (c1505), and Veronese's beautiful but fanciful *Adoration of the Magi* (c1570). The artist has transported the nativity scene out of a cattle shed and into some magnificent Roman ruins, with some rather coquettish camels and a comical dog looking on. The church also holds the tomb of Luigi da Porto and the Valmarana crypt by Palladio.

In the cloisters next door, the **Museo Naturalistico Archeologico** ⓘ *contrà Santa Corona 4, T0444-320440, Tue-Sun 0900-1700, €6.50 or €8.50 for admission to Teatro Olimpico and Museo Civico Pinacoteca, valid for 3 days,* houses a collection of Paleolithic and Roman artefacts dug up from the Berici hills, as well as some stuffed insects.

Gallerie di Palazzo Leoni Montanari

ⓘ *Contrà Santa Corona 25, T0444-578875, palazzomontanari.net. Tue-Sun 1000-1800, €5.*
This gallery exhibits a fairly comprehensive array of Russian icons and some 18th-century Venetian paintings, including those by the Guardi brothers and Pietro Longhi.

Duomo

ⓘ *Piazza Duomo, T0444-320996. Mon-Fri 1000-1200 and 1530-1730, Sat 1030-1200, Sun 1000-1200.*
Stones in the Duomo's crypt suggest that the old Roman building sited here may have been an early *domus ecclesia* or house of prayer. In the fifth century it became a Christian basilica, which was remodelled in the 11th century, then rebuilt by Lorenzo da Bologna in 1482. Palladio added a drum apse and entablature in 1557, but attaching the Pantheon-esque cupola proved rather complicated and was only completed in 1564, after he'd perfected the technique at the cathedral in Brescia. Lorenzo Veneziano's 14th-century golden altarpiece, *Dormitio Virginis* has a certain one-dimensional charm.

Palazzo Vescovile

ⓘ *Piazza Duomo 11, T0444-226300. Mon-Fri 0900-1200.*
Across the road from the cathedral is the neoclassical Palazzo Vescovile (Bishop's Palace). It has a beautiful Renaissance courtyard with big round arches called the Zeno Loggia, which was built by Bernardino da Milano in 1494.

Casa Pigafetta

① *Contrà Pigafetta.*

This ornate Gothic palazzo was built in the mid 15th century by Stefano da Ravenna and became home to Antonio Pigafetta (1480-1534), Vicenza's famous explorer. He made his name as one of only 18 survivors (out of 237 men) who returned from Magellan's expedition of 1519-22 which circumnavigated the globe. The climates, seas, amazing flowers, weird animals and strange languages they encountered are wonderfully described in Pigafetta's *La Relazione del primo viaggio intorno al mondo* (Report on the First Voyage around the World), one of the first and most authoritative texts on the geographical discoveries of the 16th century. There is no public access to this building but still much to admire from the outside, including the old French motto above the door: '*Il n'est rose sans espine*' ('there is no rose without thorns').

A stroll through Palladio's legacy

Inside the city walls (built by the Veronese della Scala family who ran things until the Venetians showed up in 1404), corso Andrea Palladio is the main thoroughfare and, running east to west, is the original central axis of the town's Roman *decumanus maximus*. A walk along the corso is a good way to discover the architectural wealth bequeathed by Palladio and continued by his protégé Vincenzo Scamozzi.

Begin at the west end in **Giardini Salvi**, a peaceful public park where the hexastyle doric **Loggia Valmarana** sits astride the Seriola stream. The *centro storico* begins at porta Castello. As you enter the piazza, far to the right is the rather faded **Palazzo Porto Breganze**, built by Scamozzi soon after his master's death in 1580. It represents just a slice of the building designed by Palladio, which had seven bays rather than the two Scamozzi completed.

On the right-hand side as you start along corso Palladio is the stately **Palazzo Thiene Bonin Longare** ① *corso A Palladio 12, May-Sep Wed-Fri 0900-1200 and 1500-1800, Sat 0900-1200, Oct-Apr Tue-Wed 0900-1200 and 1500-1800*, which is made of brick not stone (Palladio was experimenting). It was started by Palladio in 1562 and completed by Scamozzi in 1593. The building now houses the Banca Popolare Vicentina but is open on certain days to allow visitors to see the frescoes by Paolo Guidolini and Giacomo Chiesa. Further along, **Palazzo Capra-Clementi** ① *corso A Palladio 45*, built in 1540, would have been a good example of the young Palladio's work if the various owners had not tampered with the façade.

If you turn right down contra Battisti, you'll come to the Duomo (see page 39); instead, turn left along corso Fogazzaro to reach **Palazzo Valmarana Braga Rosa** ① *corso Antonio Fogazzaro 16, T392-656868, palazzovalmaranabraga.it, Wed 1000-1200 and 1500-1800*, completed by Palladio in 1565. Tightly packed into a street of houses that were once all owned by the Valmarana family, its huge arched doorway and imposing cornice make it stand out from the others. It was bombed during World War Two but the interior has been restored and there's some nice stucco work and frescoes inside, if you have a free half hour on a Wednesday.

Back on corso Palladio, if you head right down corso Cavour, it will take you to piazza dei Signori for the Basilica Palladiana and Loggia del Capitaniato (see page 37) or you can turn left onto contrà Porti to find **Palazzo Barbarano Porto** at No 11. Built by Palladio in 1571 for the nobleman Montano Barbarano, it is the only city palazzo that Palladio completed. Palladio's desire for symmetry was severely tested on this difficult site but he succeeded in creating a unified building. It now houses the **Centro Internazionale di Studi di Architettura Andrea Palladio and Museo Palladio** ① *T0444-323014, Tue-Sun 1000-1800,*

€5, €3 concessions. Many of Palladio's original drawings were bought by Lord Burlington (the 'Apollo of the Arts') and taken to London but there are still some to see here. Also on contrà Porti, at No. 15, is the house where Luigi da Porto, considered to be the author of the original version of *Romeo and Juliet*, lived and died in 1529 (he is buried in Chiesa di Santa Corona). **Palazzo Iseppo da Porto** ① *contrà Porti 21*, was built in 1552 and is one of Palladio's first palazzi.

Return to corso Palladio and then turn left onto contrà San Gaetano Thiene. The historical seat of Banca Popolare Vicentina is **Palazzo Thiene** ① *contrà San Gaetano Thiene 11, T0444-339989, palazzothiene.it, Sep-Jun Wed-Fri 0900-1700, Sat 0900-1200, Oct-Apr Tue-Wed 0900-1200 and 1500-1800*. Although the designs for this palazzo appear in Palladio's *Quattri Libri dell'Architettura*, the building doesn't look like one of Palladio's creations. It is believed that Palladio merely supervised the architect Giulio Romano on this project.

Take the next left off corso Palladio to reach Chiesa di Santa Corona (see page 39), which houses the **Valmarana crypt**, designed by Palladio as an elegant and fitting tribute to his loyal patron. Further up contrà Santa Corona is **Palazzo Leoni Montanari** (see page 39).

Back on corso Palladio you'll see the lovely little balconies and loggias of **Palazzo dal Toso Franceschini da Schio** at No 147. The building is referred to as Ca' d'Oro because of its similarity to the famous Venetian palazzo. Finally, the walk ends with a look at Palladio's modest former home at No 163, although you could carry on a little further to the **Teatro Olimpico** (see page 37), one of Palladio's masterpieces.

Santuario di Monte Berico

① *Viale X Giugno 87, T0444-559411, monteberico.it. Oct-Mar 0600-1230 and 1430-1800, Apr-Sep 0600-1230 and 1430-1900. Bus: 8 Viale Roma.*
Don't miss the short and beautiful hike up Monte Berico to visit this church. Setting off from the eastern corner of campo Marzio and onto viale X Giugno, cross the bridge and follow the signs up the hill. You'll walk along a cypress-lined path and pass a number of shrines. The Santuario was built in honour of the Madonna who appeared in 1426 then again in 1428 to advise that if the locals built a church here, Vicenza would be saved from the plague. They took her advice and the city was spared, so on 8 September every year, the locals process up this path to thank the Madonna for her good counsel.

On reaching the church, soak up the views from piazza della Vittoria before venturing inside. The domed Baroque basilica we see now was built by Carlo Borrello in 1688 and contains two artworks that are worth closer inspection: Bartolomeo Montagna's *Pietà* (1505), which despite its rudimentary style emotively conveys Mary's grief, and Veronese's *The Great Supper of St Gregory the Great* (1572). The composition of this painting echoes the artist's *Feast in the House of Levi* that hangs in the Accademia in Venice but, in this picture, the Pope takes centre stage and Jesus, dressed as a pilgrim, is placed on his right-hand side. During the occupation of the Veneto in 1848, Austrian troops slashed the canvas in a frenzied attack, tearing it to shreds, but it has since been totally reconstructed and restored. In the sacristy there are three intricate wood-inlaid closets by Pier Antonio dell'Abate da Modena: the one showing a bird in a cage is particularly delightful.

Villa Valmarana ai Nani

① *Via dei Nani 28, T0444-321803, villavalmarana.com. Mar-Oct Sat-Sun 1000-1200 and 1400-1600, €10. Bus: 8 Viale Roma or €10 in a taxi from the centro storico.*
Believe it or not, this villa is not by Palladio! It was commissioned by Giovanni Bertoli, who bequeathed it to his daughter, a nun in Padua, meaning it became the property of her

convent. Giustino Valmarana bought the villa in 1715 and the architect Francesco Muttoni developed it further. There are actually three buildings within the large gardens: the *palazzina* (main villa), completed in 1669, and the *foresteria* (guest house) and *scuderia* (stables), both of which were built around 1720.

The '*ai nani*' in the villa's name refers to the 17 dwarves with attitude that line the boundary wall. They were carved by Francesco Uliaco, who allegedly worked from some drawings by Tiepolo. It was a Baroque conceit to incorporate dwarves into the decoration of buildings and these are some of the most spirited you will find. There's a popular belief that the Valmarana family had a daughter of restricted height and hoped that the presence of these statues and a number of staff who also had physical abnormalities might ensure she felt normal.

The reason this villa is so celebrated is because of the magnificence and inventiveness of its frescoes by the Venetian painter Giambattista Tiepolo (1724-1804) and his son Giandomenico. They were commissioned by Giustino Valmarana in 1757 and have a dreamlike palette and use of perspective that pulls you in. You can tell by the colour and ingenuity of the frescoes, inspired by classical love stories and literature, that Tiepolo's imagination was given a free rein here. In the entrance hall of the *palazzina* is a remarkable portrayal of Iphigenia in Aulis (from the Greek play by Euripides), framed by architectural features. The four rooms off the hall host scenes from Homer's *Iliad*, Virgil's *Aeneid*, *Orlando Furioso* by Ludovico Ariosto and *Gerusalemme Liberata* by Torquato Tasso, an epic poem based on the first crusade.

Tiepolo gave each of the five rooms in the *foresteria* a different theme: peasants working the land throughout the seasons; China; carnival cherubs; Olympus; and 'the room of the loggia' (decorated by Girolamo Mengozzi and Antonio Visentini). These frescoes nearly ended up in Paris, but it wasn't Napoleon who sought to plunder them, it was Mussolini, who wanted them for the embassy there. Thankfully, Giustino Valmarana, who was a Christian Democrat Senator, and Giuseppe Bottai, one of Il Duce's right-hand men, managed to persuade him to leave them. The Valmarana family still own the villa and *foresteria*.

La Rotonda (Villa Almerico Capra Valmarana)
ⓘ *Via Rotonda 29, T0444-321793. Mar-Nov Tue-Sun 1000-1200 and 1500-1800, gardens only €5, gardens and villa (only Wed and Sat), €10. Bus: 8 Viale Roma (infrequent); €10 in a taxi from the centro storico.*

Connected to the Villa Valmarana ai Nani by way of a pleasant shady path, La Rotonda was commissioned in 1566 by the wealthy Vicentine cleric, Paolo Almerico, as a summer pavilion. The design is a simple square, with a dome and four identical porticos of the Ionic order on each side, which overlook the countryside. Inside, the symmetry continues with the central dome and four corridors leading to each of the porticos. Palladio took great pride in the way the landscape, materials, location, symmetrical forms and mathematical precision came together in such beauteous harmony. He died before it was finished but, once more, Scamozzi completed the work, flattening the original design of the dome. The frescoes inside are by Alessandro Maganza and Louis Dorigny, with stuccoes by Agostino Rubini and Domenico Fontana. La Rotunda has been copied numerous times; there are versions of it as far away as Delhi and Washington. It was also used as the film set for Joseph Losey's *Don Giovanni* in 1979.

North of Vicenza

Villa Porto-Colleoni-Thiene
ⓘ *Via Garibaldi 2, Thiene, T0445-366015, castellodithiene.com. Tours: Mid Mar-mid Nov Sun 1500, 1600 and 1700, €8, €5 under 13s. 20 km north of Vicenza on the S349.*
Often called the Castello, this villa was never actually a castle but certainly resembles one. It is believed to be the work of Domenico da Venezia who worked with Palladio on the Duomo and the Palazzo della Ragione between 1448 and 1453. Entered by a loggia with five huge arches, the solid rectangular structure contains a vast atrium. Francesco Porto inherited the villa in 1507 and raised the roof, adding two symmetrical white marble staircases at either side of the loggia. He also developed the gardens which to this day are kept in the Renaissance style.

The villa is celebrated for its frescoes by Veronese's top pupils Battista Zelotti (1526-1578) and Giovanni Antonio Fasolo (1530 -1572). They did their master proud with their depictions of classical mythology on the walls of the hall. At either side of the fireplace crouch Vulcan and Venus with Cupid in her arms. Bands of cherubs, bundles of fruit and sheep skulls line the cornices of the four walls, which show scenes from Roman history: the meeting of Massinissa and Sofonisba after the Roman victory over Carthage; Muzio Scevola standing defiant in front of the Etruscan King Porsenna; a blonde Cleopatra turning against Augustus; and the freeing of a lady from Carthage at Scipione.

Also worth a look are the stables downstairs. These were designed by Francesco Muttoni (1668-1747) and have mosaic cobbled floors and red marble columns with carved *putti* (cherubs) on top.

Marostica
ⓘ *14 km east of Thiene on the S248.*
This compact medieval town was formerly celebrated for its cherries but now it's famous for a human chess game, which is held on the second weekend of September in even years. After World War Two, Vucetich Mirko wrote a play in which two suitors, Renaldo and Vieri, fell in love with Lionora, the beautiful daughter of the local lord. To win her hand they challenged each other to a duel but the lord of Marostica didn't want to lose either of them, so instead he ordered the love rivals to play a chess game in the town square: whoever won would marry Lionora while the loser would marry her younger sister, Oldrada. So, the joy of chess is celebrated, avoiding bloodshed and hurt feelings and providing the opportunity for some pomp, dancing and fireworks. Some visitors feel a bit cheated when they realise there is no historical basis to the story and it is just fictional medievalism, but it has done wonders for tourism in the town and gives the locals a chance to dress up in 14th-century costume.

If you can't make it to the chess game itself, visit the **Museo dei Costumi e delle Armi della Partita a Scacchi** ⓘ *Castello Inferiore, piazza Castello, T0424-72127, daily 0900-1200 and 1500-1800, €2.50*, which displays the lavish costumes and weaponry that are worn by the chess pieces, Lionora, the king, the knights, the foot soldiers and so on: heavy doublet, hose and leg-of-mutton sleeves for the fellows and brightly coloured *bliauds* (tunics) with wimples for the ladies. The museum is housed in the town's lower castle on the main piazza, which is linked to another castle on the hill (Castello Superiore) by means of crenellated walls that fully enclose the town.

Bassano del Grappa

The green and fruitful area at the foot of Monte Grappa, where the river Brenta opens out onto the plains, has been inhabited by settlers since the Bronze Age. More recently it was the site of wartime heroics, when the Italians routed the Austrians in 1917-18, thanks to the Alpini, elite mountain soldiers who fought an unrelenting battle in the most difficult and dangerous conditions up in the Grappa. Their bravery is referenced throughout Bassano del Grappa with the tricolore and their motif cap with a feather. Three of the five Alpini brigades were disbanded after the Cold War ended but even those who are no longer in the army still consider themselves Alpini *in congedo* or 'on leave'. Every year, in late spring, members of the Associazione Nazionale Alpini gather together for a *veci* (reunion) in one of the towns in the area (the Bassano reunion is always the most trumpeted) to commemorate lost friends, drink and sing. You might not understand a word of *La Montanara* but hearing the men's voices and watching their chests puff with pride is a moving experience.

Bassano is best known for its grappa, the intense liquor made from the leftovers of wine production. The town is also famous for its majolica ceramics and white asparagus (see page 48).

Ponte Vecchio

Bassano town sits on either side of the river Brenta, linked by this sturdy, covered wooden bridge (also known as the ponte degli Alpini). Originally designed by Palladio in 1569, it has been destroyed a number of times by combat and flash floods but, apart from some tweaking by engineers to increase its strength, it remains true to the architect's vision. You can see still see evidence of the battles that have been fought here: bullet holes riddle the walls of buildings at either end of the bridge.

Museo Civico

ⓘ *Piazza Garibaldi, T0424-519901. Tue-Sat 0900-1830, Sun 1500-1800, €4.50, €3 under 14s and students, includes admission to Museo della Ceramica.*

In the cloisters of the 14th-century church of San Francesco are some Roman artefacts and some paintings by the Da Ponte or Bassano family, Jacopo and Francesco. There is also a room devoted to Canova and one to Tito Gobbi, a local baritone made good.

Museo della Ceramica

ⓘ *Palazzo Sturm, via Schiavonetti, T0424-519940. Tue-Sat 0900-1300 and 1500-1800, Sun 1530-1830, €4.50, €3 concessions, includes admission to Museo Civico.*

The majolica of Bassano has been famous in ceramic circles since the 16th century, so, if you delight in decorative dishes, this is a good place to spend an hour or so. For those less interested in ceramics, the palazzo itself has some charming frescoes, rococo rooms and lovely views over the river.

Museo degli Alpini

ⓘ *Taverna Bar Alpini, via Angarano 2, ponte Vecchio, T0424-503662. Tue-Sun 0830-2000.*

A room of the pub is dedicated to the feathered *fratelli* and shows some heart-rending photographs and relics of their icy heroics.

Poli-Museo della Grappa

ⓘ *Distillerie Poli, via Gamba 6, T0424-524426. Daily 0900-1930.*

The almost-gripping story of grappa is told in a super-smooth way in this commercial museum. Invariably, you wait for a taste of the good stuff, which is not always forthcoming.

Grotte di Oliero

ⓘ *Via Oliero di Sotto 85, Valstagna, T0424-558250, grottedioliero.it. Visit the website for opening hours and out of season bookings, €7.50, €5.50 under 15s. 14 km from Bassano on the SS47 turn left to Campolongo bridge and follow the signs to 'Grotte di Oliero'.*

The subterranean waters of the Oliero springs were discovered in 1822 by Alberto Parolini. A winding track takes you down a hill and under Rock Rampion to paths that surround the underground lake. The ground can be slippery and it can feel rather chilly, so make sure you are properly shod and clothed. Tools, discovered in the *Covolo degli Assassini* (Cave of the Murderers) show that it was once inhabited; there are also signs that a two-storey house was once tucked into the crevices. There are three other caves: the Sisters' Cave, Lord's Cave and Parolini Cave; each more difficult to reach than the last. A boat takes you to the Parolini Cave, which is an other-worldly 14-m high chamber of alabastrine stalactites. It is also home to the olm, an amphibian troglobiont or cave salamander that is native to Croatia. Parolini introduced them as an experiment and they live here quite happily.

The park above offers some lush meanderings amongst flora and fauna indigenous to the region. Also here is the **Museo di Speleologia e Carsismo**, which lovers of geology and speleology might enjoy. It has a nice little café and benches for picnics.

Vicenza and around listings

For hotel and restaurant price codes and other relevant information, see pages 11-14.

○ Where to stay

Vicenza *p37, map p38*

€€ Campo Marzio, *Viale Roma 21, T0444-545700, hotelcampomarzio.com.* You'll either love the '70s vibe of the brown reception area at this business hotel or it will make you wince. Either way, if you have booked a superior room, not to worry: they are much fresher, lighter and altogether more delightful. There are 35 rooms in total and the location is very convenient: right between the station and the historical centre and close to the buses that run to the outlying villas and hills.

€ Albergo Due Mori, *Contrà di Rode 26, T0444-321686, hotelduemori.com.* Bang in the centre of things, just a short shuffle from piazza dei Signori, this beautifully refurbished palazzo has 30 spacious rooms (27 are en suite) which are decorated in neutral tones and furnished in an art nouveau style. Breakfast is €7 extra but is well worth it. There is also a lift for those who don't want to heave their bags up the stairs.

€ Bob and Jenny's Bed and Breakfast, *Borgo Berga 140, T0444-320884, bed-breakfast-italy.com.* This B&B is located in a lovely little neighbourhood in the Berici Hills, just a gentle amble away from the Santuario di Monte Berico and a stroll from some great bars and restaurants. The family that run it are hugely engaging and offer a whole host of information on what to do, how to get there and where to eat and drink. They will also do pick-ups from the station. There are two bedrooms and a two-night minimum stay.

Self-catering
€€ Villa Pasini, *Via Roma 4, Arcugnano, nr Vicenza, T0444-270054, villapasini.com.* Tucked away in the hills between olive groves and vineyards, this spectacular villa is run by a Californian woman, Cynthia. The three chic bedrooms are accessed through a courtyard and are actually suites with small kitchenettes so you can make your own supper. Breakfast, which is included, is served outside in summer or in your room during cooler months. The rural location suits those with a car; a taxi from the city centre will set you back €12.

Bassano del Grappa *p44*
€€ Al Castello, *Via Bonamigo 19, T0424-228665.* Not far from the ponte Alpini, this small hotel has 11 variously sized rooms, all with simple but good quality wooden furnishings and spotless bathrooms. It's run by a mother and son who delight in making everything *'buona'*.vThe breakfast room may be small but it caters for big appetites (good value for an extra €8) and there is a bar downstairs with seats outside for aperitivi hour.

❼ Restaurants

Vicenza *p37, map p38*
€€€ Amici Miei Restaurant & Drinks, *Piazza Biade 6, T0444-321061, amicimiei. vi.it. Mon 1830-2400, Tue-Sat 1130-1500 and 1830-2400.* This upmarket bar is adorned with photos of the Vicentini glitterati. An aperitivo from the huge wine and drinks list (including bizarre-coloured cocktails) helps you settle into the chic, modish surroundings. Simple knock-out dishes include *penne con salsa di asparagi* (pasta with asparagus) and *gelato alla zenzero* (ginger ice cream). And, what could be better than stumbling full-bellied and merry out of here into the majesty of piazza dei Signori?

€€€ Antico Guelfo, *Contrà Pedemuro San Biagio 92, T0444 547897 anticoguelfo. it.* Serious foodies and the plain old adventurous will be in awe of the mother and daughter who dream up such imaginatively knee-weakening dishes such as strudel filled with donkey meat and wild mushrooms or rigatoni with *radicchio* and almonds. This is not a cheap eat but the food and the wines will be memorable. On the road that runs parallel to Corso Palladio, it's an easy stumble back to your hotel.

€€€ Hisyou, *Piazza delle Erbe 9, T0444-321044. Mon 1930-2400, Tue-Sun 1200-1500 and 1930-2400.* Opening a sushi restaurant in the shadow of the basilica in the heart of Vicenza must have been a huge gamble but it has paid off: the locals can't get enough of the sashimi and tappanyakis. The minimalist utility decor and gentle lighting create an unassuming atmosphere. Sapporo beer and saki make a nice change from Valpolicella, too.

€ Antica Casa della Malvasia, *Contrà delle Morette 5, T0444-543704. Tue-Sun 1130-1500 and 1830-2300.* Palladio might have designed Vicenza but in this, the city's oldest restaurant, you can eat the food that built the Vicentini. Big fat *bigoli con l'anatra* (pasta with duck sauce) and the fabulously stewy *baccalà alla Vicentina*. It's superb value for money and well suited to those who want to get stuck in to the local wines, as it has over 80 different bottles to choose from.

€ Righetti, *Piazza Duomo 3, T0444-543135. Mon-Fri 1200-1430 and 1900-2200.* This place might be self-service but the food goes way beyond cafeteria fare. With lashings of pasta, a good selection of grilled meat and vegetables, and risotto on Tuesday and Friday evenings, there is much to keep even the biggest fusspot happy. The mix of locals, including finely clad ladies, proves that this is one of the most popular eateries in Vicenza. You can sit inside or out.

Cafés and bars

Caffè Natura, *Via Battisti 17, T0444-234372. Tue-Sun 0800-2000.* If you've had your fill of coffee, this place sells beautiful smoothies and fruit-studded cakes that are so fresh tasting you could fool yourself into thinking they were good for you.

Galla Caffé, *Corso Palladio 11, T0444-225200 Sun-Mon 0900-1500, Tue-Thu 0900-2000, Fri-Sat 0900-2400.* Right on the main drag, this friendly bar has an arty, bookish crowd that head upstairs for readings or classical music.

Gran Caffè Garibaldi, *Via Cavour 7, T0444-544147. Wed-Mon 0900-2400.* Sitting outside on the piazza drinking cappuccino in this notable café is an unmissable Vicenza experience. And you won't have to move either as they serve lunch and dinner too. Upstairs is posh and rather expensive but worth a peek.

Il Grottino, *Piazza della Erbe 2. Daily 1700-0200.* Right behind the basilica, this bar is open every night for apertivi, snacks and music.

Osteria Ca' d'Oro, *Contrà San Gaetano da Thiene 8, T0444-323713. Daily 1200-1430 and 1900-2230.* Close to the palazzo that resembles Venice's Ca' d'Oro, this bar is popular with a young crowd and with those who think they are young. Great food, modestly priced.

Ovosodo, *Contrà Pescherie Vecchie 12, T0444-235315 Tue-Sun 0900-0200.* Beautiful contemporary wine bar that spills out on to one of the streets behind Piazza Dei Signori.

Pasticceria Sorarù, *Piazzetta Palladio 17, T0444-320915. Thu-Tue 0830-1300 and 1530-2000.* Whether you're inside amongst the columns, marble and mirrors or outside watching the stylish Vicentini stride by, you'll find the coffee and artisan pastries are as good as the surroundings.

Bassano del Grappa *p44*

€€ Osteria Terraglio, *Piazza Terraglio 28, T0424-521064. Tue-Sun 0830-1500 and 1700-0200.* This rustic restaurant packs them in and is one of the most spirited places in town. The menu runs the whole gamut: juicy salads, cured meats, roasted vegetables (including the local white asparagus), grilled fish and pasta with robust sauces. There are lots of wines to choose from, too, but you don't have to flash your cash as the house white is most enjoyable. Tuesday is jazz night.

Cafés and bars

Bar Paninoteca al Porton, *Via Gamba 3, T0424-524079. Mon 0800-1430, Wed-Sun 0800-2400.* The chunky wooden benches outside and the flowers in the window boxes give this a jolly, Alpine, beer-drinking atmosphere. Great coffee and fulsomely filled panini.

🎧 Entertainment

Vicenza *p37, map p38*
Cinema
Cinema Odeon, *Corso A Palladio 186, T0444-543492. Tue-Sun 2000.* Come here for the usual Hollywood fare dubbed into Italian. Independent and arthouse films also occasionally feature on the bill.

Cinema Teatro Araceli, *Borgo Scrofa 20, T0444-514253.* Cinema buffs will love the traditional cinema experience and the singular line-up of classic movies.

Clubs
Totem Club, *Via Vecchia Ferriera 166, T0444-291176. Sat 2230-0400.* To the west of the city, this club holds avant-garde, house and Gothic industrial nights and entertains a mainly studenty, alternative crowd.

Villa Bonin, *Viale del Commercio 8, T0444-348168. Wed, Fri-Sat 2300-0400.* Near the Fiera on the other side of the train line, this mammoth bar, club and restaurant is a rather slick operation and full of the most gorgeous people you'll have ever seen: '*Megabella!*'

Theatre

Teatro Olimpico, *Piazza Matteotti 11, T0444-222800, olimpicovicenza.it.* For information on performances and ticketing, contact the tourist information office in piazza Matteotti. Tickets €10-40. Can there be a more amazing venue to experience a live performance? There's a jazz festival in May, orchestral works in June and drama (tending on the classical side) in September and October.

⊙ Shopping

Vicenza *p37, map p38*
Art and antiques

An antiques market is held in piazza dei Signori on the second Sunday of every month. The items are all quite randomly displayed but there are some joys to behold: a glove stretcher in the shape of a bird's beak, for instance.

Books

Libreria Montesello Anna, *Contrà San Gaetano Thiene 2a, T0444-326103. Mon-Sat 0930-1300 and 1600-1900.* Some fascinating discoveries can be made in this small but satisfying little bookshop.

Clothing and accessories

The whole of corso Palladio is lined with high-street clothes shops, including Zara, H&M, Bata, Conbipel, Golden Point (socks and tights), Sephora (make up and perfume), Intimissini (undies), Max & Co, and others.

Department stores

Coin, *Piazza Castello 190, T0444-546044. Mon 1530-1930, Tue-Fri and Sun 1000-1300 and 1530-1930, Sat 1000-1300 and 1530-2000.* Good old trusty Coin: always there when you need new flip flops, pants, make-up, shorts, etc.

Food and drink

Dolci Tentazioni, *Corso A Palladio 23,* *T0444-700245, dtdolcitentazioni.it. Mon-Sat 0900-1300 and 1500-1930.* Fabulous chocolates, honey and different flavoured salts and peppers.

Il Ceppo Gastronomia, *Corso A Palladio 196, T0444-544414, gastronomiailceppo.com. Mon-Sat 0900-1300 and 1500-1900.* The best quality and most comprehensive selection of carry-out cold dishes, bread, cheese and salami you will find in Vicenza: perfect for picnics. You can also take goodies home with you in vacuum packs, such as a slice of Bastardo del Grappa (a much-loved local cheese).

Piaceri e Peccati, *Corso A Palladio 150, T0444-327417, piaceriepeccati.it. Mon-Sat 0930-1300 and 1500-1930.* Purveyors of fine sweeties, herbs, oils, jams: indeed, all things tasty.

Gifts

Cartoleria Zamperetti, Corso A Palladio 66, T0444-321265. Mon-Sat 0930-1300 and 1500-1900. Pretty coloured paper, envelopes and leather-bound books.

Bassano del Grappa *p44*
Food and drink

Bassano del Grappa is famous for its *asparago bianco* (white asparagus), which has been cultivated underground in this area since the 15th century. It can be found in abundance in fruit and vegetable markets all over Veneto from the last week in April until 13 June. There is considerable pride amongst the growers of these spears and the last harvest is always announced, so that customers know that anything they buy thereafter must have been refrigerated and will therefore have an impaired flavour.

Thursday is market day in Bassano and a great opportunity to buy some dried mushrooms and beans to take home.
Il Melario, *Via Angaro 13, T0424-502168, ilmelario.it. Daily 0900-1300 and 1500-1900.* There is an amazing array of dried mushrooms and beans for sale here, as well as grappa galore.

ⓞ What to do

Vicenza and around *p37, map p38*

Cultural tours

Veneto Tours (T349-1016700, theothersideofvenice.com) offer a great day-long Palladian tour of Vicenza, either on foot or chauffeur-driven, from €200 for two people. Their passion for Palladio make their tours of his palazzi and villas particularly insightful: perfect if you only have a day in the area and want to pack as much in as possible.

Cycling

Dolcevita Bike Tours (T070-920 9885, dolcevitabiketours.com) run a great seven-day self-guided tour of the Veneto starting from Vicenza. The route heads past a number of the most famous villas (including the splendid Villa Barbaro) to Marostica, Asolo, Bassano del Grappa, Treviso, Venice, Chioggia and Padua, before returning to Vicenza. It's a comprehensive and not too hilly route. For around €800 you'll get an orientation session before you go, accommodation, meals, baggage transfer, all road maps and, of course, a bike.

⊖ Transport

Vicenza and around *p37, map p38*

Local buses are provided by **AIM**: useful routes include bus 13, which stops near La Rotonda and Villa Valmarana ai Nani, and bus 18, which goes up to Santuario di Monte Berico. **FTV** buses serve regional destinations, including Vicenza to Thiene

to Vicenza (bus 15); Thiene to Marostica to Bassano del Grappa to Thiene (bus 44); Vicenza to Marostica to Bassano del Grappa to Vicenza (no.5). Also buses from viale Milano to Venice (1 hr) Padua (50 mins) and Verona (1 hr 40 mins); and to Thiene (20 mins), Marostica (30 mins) and Bassano del Grappa (1 hr).

FTV (T0444-223111, ftv.vi.it) is based next to the train station at viale Milano 78.

The train station, **Vicenza Stazione FS**, is on piazzale della Stazione, campo Marzio, T0444-325046, trenitalia.it. Hourly train services to Milan (2 hrs 30 mins) Venice (50 mins), Padua (20 mins) and Verona (30-45 mins).

Taxis are available from piazza la Stazione and via Lago di Levico 11.

ⓞ Directory

Vicenza and around *p37, map p38*

Money There are a number of ATMs on corso A Palladio. **Medical services Ospedale di Vicenza**, viale Ferdinando Rodolfi 1, T0444-753111. **Farmacia Al Redentor**, piazza delle Erbe 21, T0444-321951 (Mon-Sat 0930-1230 and 1330-1930); **Farmacia Centrale Valeri**, corso A Palladio 136, T0444-321964 (Mon-Sat 0900-1300 and 1600-1700). **Post office** Piazza Garibaldi Giuseppe 1, T0444-322468 (Mon-Sat 0830-1830). **Tourist information** Piazza Matteotti 12, T0444-320854, vicenzae.org (daily 0900-1300 and 1400-1800); piazza dei Signori 8, T0444-544122 (daily 1000-1400 and 1430-1830).

Contents

Footprint features

Lake Garda

Lake Garda is Italy's largest lake and while it's popular with retired couples and those in the mood for romance, it's also a favourite with sporting enthusiasts and families. Theme parks, grand hotels, spas, excellent restaurants, as well as superb sailing and windsurfing are all on offer – and all are set amidst some spectacular scenery, particularly at the north of the lake. Sirmione, on the southern shore, is perhaps the most photographed town here because of its magnificent castle with a real moat and drawbridge. Spas, restaurants, shopping and Roman ruins are the attractions at Sirmione – although kids will probably want to head to nearby Gardaland, considered to be the best theme park in Italy. Heading clockwise, we pass the pretty town of Salò where Mussolini retreated to on the lake's west coast, and Gardone Riviera where Il Vittoriale, an ostentatious villa once owned by Italy's famously eccentric poet Gabriele d'Annunzio, is to be found. The northern end of the lake is where the sailing action is concentrated, and where everything from dinghies to yachts can be found tacking with a backdrop of spectacular mountains that work as a wind tunnel, providing reliable gusts almost every day. Riva del Garda and Torbole are the favourite haunts of sailing types, as is Malcesine on the eastern side of the lake.

Southern Lake Garda

The southern shore – Basso Garda to the locals – is the most tourist-focused, attracting hordes of tourists to Sirmione for its castle and Roman sights, and to Peschiera del Garda for its nearby theme parks.

Sirmione → *For listings, see pages 55-58.*

Little more than a slender finger poking into Lake Garda, Sirmione is undeniably stunning. From the moment you see the spectacular castle at its entrance and enter the village across a wooden drawbridge, you imagine you're in for a treat. Once inside, however, unless you're here early or late in the season (March or October), it's sheer chaos, the pedestrian streets of the village teeming with tourists, the crush especially overwhelming at the height of summer. Prepare yourself for the crowds of sunburnt tourists slurping Sirmione's famous over-sized gelato cones and your risk of disappointment is lowered. Stay here overnight and spend the day sunning yourself on the lake and only slip out at night (when the daytrippers have gone) to explore the village's labyrinthine streets, lined with cafés and elegant boutiques (and, naturally, store after store selling tourist trinkets), and you'll find Sirmione considerably more charming.

Rocca Scaligera
ⓘ *Piazza Castello, T030-916468. Mar-Oct Tue-Sun 0830-1900, Nov-Feb Tue-Sun 0830-1700, €5.*
Kids (or the big kids in all of us) love Sirmione's 13th-century stone citadel, with its crenellated walls, squat towers, drawbridges and moats that are the stuff of fairytales. Strategically located and splendidly preserved, the castle served as a fortress as late as the 19th century. Built by the Verona-based della Scala dynasty, who constructed many of the splendid fortresses in this region, it was seized in 1402 by the Visconti family. Once over the drawbridge to the town, you'll find a second moat and drawbridge leading to the castle itself. While the interior is not as impressive as the striking exterior, there are gorgeous views.

Grotte di Catullo
ⓘ *Via Catullo, T030-916157. Mar-Oct Tue-Sun 0830-1900, Nov-Feb Tue-Sun 0830-1700, €5.*
According to local legend, these cave-like ruins are those of the Roman villa of the pleasure-seeking poet Catullus (87-54 BC). More recent archaeological evidence suggests the ruins belonged to two villas, both dating to around the first century AD. You'll find them by walking to the very end of via Caio Valerio Catullo, then taking a left at piazzale Orti Manara, or by walking through Parco Maria Callas to Lido della Bionde and climbing up through the olive groves to the grotto. Avoid a visit in the midday sun, when the walk is a challenge in the sweltering heat as there's little shade apart from in the park. If you must, there's a small tourist train that will take you there but it's preferable to do the visit in the early morning or late afternoon.

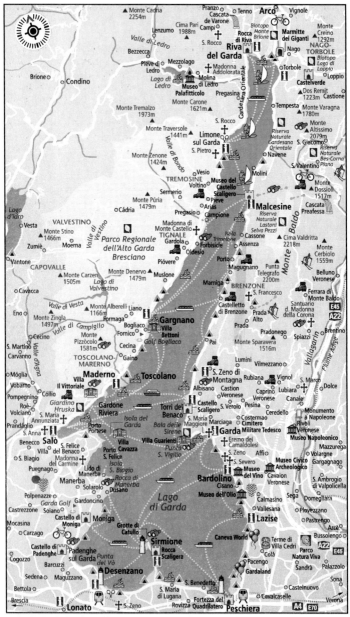

Desenzano → *For listings, see pages 55-58.*

More formally known as Desenzano del Garda, this rather delightful town on the southwestern shore of Lake Garda is the lake's largest – and busiest. While it's certainly an attractive town with its picturesque old harbour, waterfront cafés and restaurants, and 17th-century **Duomo** on piazza Malvezzi, what's most appealing about it is that it's a working town that is alive outside of the tourist season. However, this is also one of the most frustrating things about Desenzano if you're after a peaceful holiday, because the roads are heavy with traffic (especially on market days) and parking is impossible to find. It's definitely one of those towns you need to stay the night at, so you can wander the tranquil streets early morning or evening to fully appreciate it.

Villa Romana

ⓘ *Via Crocefisso 22, T030-914 3547. Mar-Oct Tue-Sun 0830-1900, €3.*
These ruins of a late imperial Roman villa, considered some of Italy's most important, give a great insight into the majestic rural estates where those with the means to do so retreated as anarchy began to spread in Rome in the fourth century AD. Built in the first century AD, the most impressive aspect of the site to the untrained eye is the beautiful decorative mosaics, although some remain only partially excavated.

Peschiera del Garda

Situated on the southeastern corner of Lake Garda, Peschiera's *centro storico*, situated within the well-preserved old walls, is worth a look if you're here to take the kids to the theme parks (see page 57), but there's little else to hold your interest. The town gets uncomfortably busy in summer, and even if you are here for the theme parks, you're better off basing yourself somewhere else on the lake.

Southern Lake Garda listings

For hotel and restaurant price codes and other relevant information, see pages 11-14.

🛏 Where to stay

Sirmione *p53, map p54*
€€€€ Hotel Sirmione, *Piazza Castello 19, T030-9904922, termedisirmione.com.* This four-star is as about as close to the crowded Castello as you want to get, but it's quite a retreat with lake-facing rooms. A fine breakfast and renowned spa, the Aquaria Club.
€€€ Flaminia Hotel, *Piazza Flaminia 8, T030-916078, hotelflaminia.it.* This elegant four-star is a friendly, family-run affair with

43 rooms in a waterfront building. Standard rooms are conservatively decorated with side views of the lake, while the superior rooms and spacious junior suites boast full lake vistas. There's a wonderful sunbathing terrace and their Ristorante Signori is a good option.
€€ Hotel Eden, *Piazza Carducci 3, T030-916481, cerinihotels.it.* It's not often that you arrive over a moat to a hotel recommended by Ezra Pound in a letter to James Joyce, but it's true in this case. Near the old town centre action, this four-star is a cosy oasis with rooms boasting views of the lake or historic pedestrian square. Friendly staff, wonderful breakfasts, unbeatable location.

Desenzano *p55, map p54*

€€€ Park Hotel, *Lungolago Cesare Battisti 19, T030-914 3494, cerinihotels.it.* This elegant four-star is the best in town, beautifully furnished in a fab location. The stylish executive rooms were renovated in 2008. Great facilities include Wi-Fi and a good restaurant. In 2009 there'll be a rooftop swimming pool. Breakfast is not included at standard prices, but hotel garage parking is free.

€€ Hotel Tripoli, *Piazza Matteotti 18, T030-914 1305, hotel-tripoli.it.* This delightful old building is home to a three-star hotel facing the waterside promenade. While the rooms don't possess the charm the façade suggests, it's still an agreeable hotel and the location is excellent. First floor lake-facing rooms boast small private balconies. Private parking 200 m away.

🍴 Restaurants

Sirmione *p53, map p54*

€€€€ La Rucola, *Via Strentelle 3, T030-916326, ristorantelarucola.it.* A refined Michelin-starred restaurant situated in streets crammed with gelaterias is quite a surprise. So is the polished seasonal Mediterranean-focused menu. Expect attentive service, a spot-on wine list, and delightful desserts.

€€€ Il Girasole, *Via Vittorio Emanuele 72, T030-919182, ilgirasole.info.* Easy to spot by its plant-covered terrace, the 'sunflower' is an elegant restaurant in one of the liveliest areas of town. The speciality is seafood, which appears throughout the menu, or for a series of local seafood tasters try the *Menù Degustazione del Lago*.

€€ Risorgimento, *Piazza Carducci 5/6, T030-916325, ristorante-risorgimento.com.* A local favourite, this restaurant has a homely interior and tables on the square in good weather. The food is mostly northern Italian and seafood is a speciality, so try their spaghetti with lobster (*spaghetti all'astice*) or their baked sea bass in salt crust.

Desenzano *p55, map p54*

€€€€ Cavallino, *Via Murachette 29, T030-912 0217, ristorantecavallino.it.* An elegant and distinctive restaurant specializing in lake fish and other highly fancied seafood such as scallops and lobster. Impressive tasting menus and fine desserts and wines.

€€€€ Esplanade, *Via Lario 10, T030-914 3361, ristorante-esplanade.net.* This Michelin-starred restaurant combines jaw-dropping lake views with equally breathtaking cuisine. The emphasis is fresh seasonal produce and the cooking is sublime, with creative touches that don't overwhelm the fine ingredients. Excellent wine list and service.

🎭 Entertainment

Lake Garda *p51, map p54*

As Lake Garda and Lake Iseo attract a combination of couples in the mood for romance, mature aged travellers, and camping families, there's little in the way of nightlife. Entertainment tends to be focused on the refined, such as a summer classical music concert, or the laid-back, quiet aperitivo at a lakeside bar or a gelato and stroll after dinner. No matter where you are on the lake come early evening in the warmer months it's time to enjoy an *aperitivo* or two, whether it's at a casual kiosk on a waterfront promenade or a swish waterside terrace at a grand hotel. After dinner, everyone heads to the nearest gelateria for an icecream and stroll by the water.

Bars

Lake Garda and Lake Iseo's towns all boast café-bars overlooking the lake or on main squares. Café-bars tend to open most days from early in the morning until late at night, with their patrons drinking coffee by day and aperitivi in the evenings. Bars that mainly operate as wine bars tend to open just before lunch and close after midnight.

◎ Shopping

Lake Garda *p51, map p54*
The shopping around Lake Garda isn't anything special. The best towns for shopping are Sirmione and Desenzano, where there are fashion boutiques, shops selling linens and silks, handpainted ceramics, pottery, glassware, souvenirs, and gourmet food and wine. Most shops open from Monday-Saturday 0930 or 1000, close for lunch at 1200 or 1300, then reopen from 1600-1900, although in Sirmione, the most touristy of Garda's towns, many shops stay open throughout the day during summer to take advantage of the huge crowds of tourists.

Markets

There are open-air street markets on in the mornings at towns and villages around the lake selling fresh produce, plants, clothes and accessories, and household items. They are usually held on the main square and surrounding pedestrian streets and are easy enough to find.

Monday: Sirmione, Peschiera del Garda, Torri del Benaco; Tuesday: Desenzano; Wednesday: Riva del Garda, Gargnano, San Felice del Benaco (near Salò); Thursday: Toscolano and Maderno; Friday: Garda, Lugana di Sirmione (south of Sirmione); Saturday: Salò, Malcesine; Sunday: Rivoltella (east of Desenzano).

◎ What to do

Lake Garda *p51, map p54*
Sport and outdoor
For watersports such as sailing, windsurfing and kite-surfing, and outdoor activities such as mountain biking, rock-climbing and walking, see page 67.
Navigazione Lago di Garda, *Piazza Matteotti, Desenzano, T030-914 9511, navigazionelaghi.it. Mar-Sep only.* The lakes' government-operated water transport service for Lake Garda offers fairly frequent

services to lake towns, and several daily full-day tourist cruises (from €17-22) departing from Desenzano for Sirmione and Gardone; Salò and Sirmione; Riva del Garda; and Peschiera and Riva del Garda. They also offer a full day Isola del Garda excursion (€35) several days a week.

Theme parks

Many Italian families base themselves at camping areas around Lake Garda so they have easy access to the various theme parks near the lake, including the Disneyland-like **Gardaland** (gardaland. it), **Movieland** (movieland.it), **Medieval Times** (medievaltimes.it), **Sea Life Aquarium** (seaeurope.com), **AquaParadise** (aquaparadise.it), **Il Parco Acquatico Cavour** (parcoacquaticocavour.it), **Jungle Adventure** (jungleadventure.it), and the animal safari park called **Parco Natura Viva** (parconaturaviva.it). You can drive to these, which gives you greater flexibility (after all, these are not Disneyland), or do a tour (see below).

Themed tours

Sirmione ProLoco tourist office, *at entrance to centro storico, T030-919322, comune.sirmione.bs.it.* In conjunction with the Hotels and Restaurants Association, Sirmione ProLoco offers an array of interesting guided tours in Sirmione and around Lake Garda, from history and archaeological-themed tours to wine-tasting tours such as **A Glass of History**, which includes visits to the best wineries in the area.

Well-being

Lake Garda boasts a number of thermal spas, but the best to visit is **Aquaria** (piazza Don A Piatti 1, T030-916044, termedisirmione.com), which boasts swimming pools, whirlpools, and myriad spa treatments, from massage to aromatherapy.

⊖ Transport

Southern Lake Garda *53, map p54*
Bus station, Via Marconi 26, Desenzano.
Desenzano also has a train station, which is
reached from the bus station.

❶ Directory

Sirmione *p53, map p54*
Money ATMs opposite entrance to Rocca
Scaligera. **Medical services** **Azienda**
Ospedaliera Di Desenzano Del Garda,
via Monte Croce, Desenzano Del Garda,
T030-91451. **Farmacia Internazionale
Di Cornacchione Arnaldo**, via S. Maria
Maggiore 18, T030-916004 (Mon-Wed, Fri-
Sun 0945-1215 and 1630-1900, Thu 0945-
1215). **Post office** Largo Faselo Bitinico
1, T030-916195 (Mon-Fri 0830-1400, Sat
0830-1230). **Tourist information** Viale G
Marconi 2, T030-916114 (Mon, Wed, Thu
0900-1200 and 1500-1900, Tue and Fri
0900-1200), sirmionebs.it.

Western Lake Garda

The area on the western shore, north of Desenzano (known as the Valtenesi) is an idyllic area of gently undulating hills dotted with olive groves. The main road lies inland; however, there are a couple of diversions on the way worth a quick peek including Moniga, which has a pretty harbour, and the area around Manerba, where there are picturesque beaches. The northern two-thirds of the lake, beginning around Salò, is known as the Alto Garda, or upper shore, and has a decidedly different look and feel to the south, attracting a more affluent traveller to the romantic and refined villages of Gardone Riviera and Gargnano along the mid-west shore.

Salò → For listings, see pages 61-63.

Salò is certainly a sight for sore eyes. The first glimpse you get of this genteel village skirting a gorgeous bay lined with elegant buildings and palatial art nouveau villas will have you eagerly figuring out a way to get closer for a look – which is not an easy task. When you see a parking space, grab it, as wherever you park you won't have far to walk, and a stroll here along what is arguably Italy's longest lakeside promenade, Lungolago G Zanardelli, is one of the delights of visiting Salò anyway.

Perhaps because it has few sights to speak of – the **Torre dell'Orologio** (ancient city gate) and the Gothic-Renaissance **Duomo** (0830-1900) are about all that could be considered 'attractions' – and maybe because it appeals largely to well-to-do Italians and affluent Americans, Salò is generally overlooked by English-language guidebooks, which is all the more reason to stay.

Even if you're out and about most of the day exploring the lake, you'll know your evenings will be very pleasantly spent with a promenade along the leafy lakeside, browsing the chic shops hidden within the elegant waterfront arcades, checking out the sleek yachts anchored at the marina, and kicking back in the pretty piazzas with a gelato. Try the lively piazza Dal Vittoria, where the ferry docks and where you'll find most of the cafés and restaurants. Kids also seem to enjoy thumping across the wooden boardwalks and feeding the ducks.

Gardone Riviera → For listings, see pages 61-63.

Leafy Gardone Riviera, a couple of kilometres north of Salò, was once the most glamorous resort on Lake Garda. While it's no longer fashionable, its grand old hotels with their luxuriant gardens, lakeside swimming pools and superlative restaurants still have a certain faded grandeur that make them a must-do for romantics and travellers nostalgic for the glorious early days of Grand Tour travel. After climbing up the hill to explore the charming village, eat at Agli Angeli (see page 62); amble about the verdant **Giardino Botanico Hruska** ① *T0365-20347, Mar-Oct 0900-1900, €6*, and do a tour of **Il Vittoriale**, there is little else to do except stroll along the palm-lined promenade, but that's the way most travellers like it.

Il Vittoriale

① *Via Vittoriale, Gardone di Sopra, T0365-296511, vittoriale.it. Apr-Sep 0830-2000, guided tours of house (Tue-Sun) and War Museum (Thu-Tue) 0930-1900; Oct-Mar 0900-1700, guided tours of house (Tue-Sun) and War Museum (Thu-Tue) 0900-1300 and 1400-1700. Gardens only €5, garden and tour of house/War Museum €12, garden and tour of house and War Museum €16.*

Gardone Riviera's main attraction is the magnificent Il Vittoriale, with its lavish gardens, curious war museum and whimsical villa where eccentric poet Gabriele d'Annunzio lived in the dark for 17 years – he was photophobic. A guided tour moves fairly rapidly through the many inter-connecting rooms, each decorated in a different theme or style, all crammed with a compelling jumble of art, antiques and curiosities that d'Annunzio collected.

The only way to see Il Vittoriale's interior is on a guided tour; however, tour scheduling is poorly organised. Scheduling seems to be dictated according to the guide's convenience so this means sometimes the wait is long. You can join Italian tours and read a translation collected from the locker room; bags and cameras must be stored. Otherwise, take a picnic lunch, buy your tickets, put your names down on a tour, then explore the shady gardens.

The tour begins in The Vestibule with its ancient walnut choir stalls before proceeding to two waiting rooms, one for friends, the other for unwelcome visitors like Mussolini and creditors. Next is The Music Room where pianist Luisa Baccara used to play, its fabric-draped walls resembling an Arabian tent. D'Annunzio's bedroom is probably the most fascinating room, jammed with intriguing objects, cushions, and Persian carpets, while the Blue Bathroom is probably the most cluttered you'll ever see, packed with over 900 objects. At the end of it all, you'll either be ready to scan the nearest antique market for some re-decorating when you get back home or be yearning to check into a minimalist hotel!

Spread over five terraces, the sprawling nine-hectare gardens are dotted with strange sculptures, statues, ponds and fountains, but the most unusual features must be the poet's extraordinary wedding cake monument to himself, and, below it, the navy ship embedded into the hillside; this was a memorial to two of d'Annunzio's comrades who died during their invasion of Fiume (orchestrated by d'Annunzio himself), where he and his followers set up a (short-lived) government of their own!

Gargnano → *For listings, see pages 61-63.*

More so than any other spot on the lake, lovely Gargnano, a former 13th-century Franciscan centre, seems to have its loyal devotees who return to spend their summers relaxing at this easy-going lakeside resort with its small pebble beach and tiny harbour. You can pick them out a mile away – they're the foreign travellers (many German who own villas here) who look right at home, speak enough Italian to get by, and always know all the waiters by name. Unlike Gardone Riviera, the main road runs a bit of a distance inland, leaving the waterfront area relatively tranquil and traffic-free, which is part of the reason for its popularity. Apart from stroll the tree-lined promenade, read a book from one of the many shady park benches or go sailing on the lake, there is very little to do. But, once again, like in Gardone Riviera that's exactly the way people here like it!

Four lakes' drive

From Gargnano, a turn-off takes you on an engaging edge-of-your-seat drive – be prepared for never-ending switchbacks and hairpin turns – through jaw-dropping scenery to narrow **Lago di Valvestino** deep within a lofty valley. From here the road takes you over a high pass before dropping through dense woods to the tranquil Alpine fjord-like **Lago d'Idro** – at 370 m, Lombardy's highest lake, although a pond compared to the other watery expanses, but nevertheless spectacular with steep mountains either side. Nearby, little **Bagolino** with its stone houses is a gem, while **Storo** is stunningly set beneath sheer cliffs. Once through a dramatic cleft by a rocky river and waterfall, you traverse a lush valley, **Passa Ampola**, before descending to diminutive **Lago di Ledro** surrounded by forest parks, and the lush vineyards of **Pre** to **Riva del Garda** back on the big lake.

Lake Iseo → *For listings, see pages 61-63.*

Lying west of Lake Garda, northwest of Brescia and a little under halfway to Lake Como, Lago d'Iseo, is often overlooked by visitors to Garda and Como, yet it's worth dropping into en route between lakes if you're doing a driving holiday. Lake Iseo may not boast the refined beauty of lakes Como or Orta, nor does it have the dramatic surroundings of lakes Garda or Maggiore, but its mountain setting is stunning and the waterfront at Iseo town is lovely. The lake also has a laid-back attitude many visitors find appealing. Despite the low-key vibe, it's very touristy, its camping spots and holiday resorts inundated with Italian and foreign package tourists throughout the summer months, and away from the shore the modern towns and heavy industry are unattractive.

Western Lake Garda listings

For hotel and restaurant price codes and other relevant information, see pages 11-14.

🌣 Where to stay

Salò *p59, map p54*

€€ Hotel Bellerive, *Via Pietro da Salò 11, T0365-520410, hotelbellerive.it.* Tastefully renovated, this hotel on the marina dates to 1933 – the feel is fresh and bright but still soulful. The swimming pool is just large enough for the summer crowd and the waterfront restaurant demands alfresco dining. They have villa apartments for three-day stays or longer – perfect for unwinding while watching the boats bob on the harbour.

Gardone Riviera *p59, map p54*

€€€€ Grand Hotel Fasano, *Corso Zantelli 190, T0365-290220, ghf.it.* Garda's most famous hotel offers what many believe to

be the quintessential lakeside experience. There are several price categories, with lake-view rooms being more expensive but worth every euro. Lovely gardens, fine restaurant, and the Aqva Spa make it difficult to leave. For romantics there are rooms in an old hunting lodge.

€€€€ Villa Fiordaliso, *Via Zanardelli 150, T0365-20158, villafiordaliso.it.* This pink neoclassical villa has been transformed into an exquisite hotel, the lake's most romantic. An exclusive Relais and Châteaux property with only five suites, its bragging rights go to the sumptuous 'Claretta' suite, named after Mussolini's mistress who lived here. A stay isn't complete without visiting their Michelin-starred waterfront restaurant and a drink at the piano bar atop the medieval San Marco Tower.

€€€ Gran Hotel Gardone, *Via Zanardelli 84, T0365-20261, grangardone.it.* One of the classic hotels of the region, a visit is such a time warp you half expect Churchill to be here painting, as he actually did many years ago. The fact that not much appears to have changed since will either have you excited or looking elsewhere. Splendid pool, lovely breakfast area, helpful front desk staff, but waiters are surly. Dinner is best taken elsewhere.

€€ Locanda Agli Angeli, *Piazza Garibaldi 2, T0365-20991, agliangeli.com*. Located in a lovely part of the upper town of Gardone Riviera, this is a friendly family-run hotel. All rooms have exposed beam ceilings and a pared-down elegance. The superb restaurant is a must with an outdoor terrace with tables spilling onto the atmospheric square.

Gargnano *p60, map p54*

€€€€ Hotel Villa Feltrinelli, *Via Rimembranza 38/40, T0365-798000, villafeltrinelli.com*. This beautiful villa and gardens, built by the prominent Feltrinelli family in 1892, served as some summer escape. And this was some summer shack! In 1977 noted hotelier Bob Burns bought the villa, restoring it to its former splendour – integrating historical fittings with mod cons. But it's the notion of croquet on the lawn, cocktails in the elegant bar, and pretending this is all your very own that has the greatest appeal. It's ideal for that special holiday.

€€ Hotel du Lac, *Via Colletta 21, T0365-71107, hotel-dulac.it*. Located on the water, this intimate family-run hotel has only 11 rooms. Recently renovated, six have balconies overlooking the lake while the others face the fascinating village streets. Each is decorated with local 19th or early 20th century furniture. The lovely shaded terrace, where you take breakfast, and the hotel restaurant boast water views.

Lake Iseo *p61, map p54*

€ Hotel Milano, *Lungolago G. Marconi 4, T0309-80449, hotelmilano.info*. A good option in Iseo, this hotel-restaurant has

decent rooms, some with balcony and lake views. The restaurant's summer terrace is pleasant and the food honest.

🍴 Restaurants

Salò *p59, map p54*

€€€ Gallo Rosso, *Vicolo Tomacelli 4, T036-552 0757, ristorantegallorosso.it*. Your best bet, this local favourite has earned its reputation with excellent fish and other delicious seafood dishes turned out by accomplished chefs.

€€ Osteria dell'Orologio, *Via Butturini 25, T036-529 0158*. A great choice for a casual meal, you can't go wrong with the fresh seafood and seasonal game dishes, or simply a pasta with a glass of wine. Excellent value.

Gardone Riviera *p59, map p54*

€€€€ Villa Fiordaliso, *Via Zanardelli 150, T036-520158, villafiordaliso.it*. If the hotel itself doesn't tempt you (see Where to stay), gastronomes shouldn't miss this delightful restaurant with meals served on the terrace in summer with magical views of the lake – very romantic. There's magic in the kitchen as well, as this Michelin-starred restaurant turns out highly creative seafood dishes. Their desserts are a little over the top, though, so don't be disappointed if you can't quite finish them off!

€€€ Locanda Agli Angeli, *Piazza Garibaldi 2, T0365-20832, agliangeli.com*. What appears to be a lovely eatery, with tables spilling out onto the piazza in summer, has gastronomic surprises aplenty – seasonal specials are excellent, with plenty of invention and skill. Service is warm and attentive and there's a surprisingly relaxed atmosphere, considering the quality of the cuisine.

Gargnano *p60, map p54*

€€€€ Hotel Villa Feltrinelli, *Via Rimembranza 38/40, T0365-798000, villafeltrinelli.com*. The restaurant at this

eye-poppingly pretty villa has a superb pedigree, with young chef Stefano Baiocco having worked with some of the greatest chefs of the era, such as Alain Ducasse, Pierre Gagnaire and Ferran Adrià. Everyone with a passing interest in great gastronomy should book a table to see what the fuss is about. Expect refined cuisine with fine flavours, and painstaking presentation with garnishes from the chef's garden.
€€€ La Tortuga, *Via XXIV Maggio 5, T0365-71251.* This unassuming and cosy restaurant would be fine if it offered good cuisine, but it does so much more, to the point that the restaurant has become a must-do for foodies visiting the area. This is one restaurant on the lake where meat gets as much attention as fish.

Lake Iseo *p61, map p54*
€€€ Il Paiolo, *Piazza Mazzini 9, 0309-821074.* A local favourite in the historic centre, it's gained a reputation for local dishes as well as *culatello* (the finest cut of parma ham) and other cold cuts.

🎵 Entertainment

Western Lake Garda *p59, map p54*
See page 56 for general information on entertainment around Lake Garda.

Gardone Riviera *p59, map p54*
Music, Dance, Theatre, Opera
Teatro del Vittoriale, *Via Vittoriale 12, Gardone Riviera, T036-520072,*

teatrodelvittoriale.it. An annual summer festival is hosted by this theatre in July and August with everything from opera to jazz and dance.

🛍 Shopping

Western Lake Garda *p59, map p54*
See page 57 for general information on shopping around Lake Garda, and for information on markets around Western Lake Garda.

⏰ What to do

Western Lake Garda *p59, map p54*
See page 57 for general information on What to do around Lake Garda. In the western area try:
Navigazione Lago d'Iseo, *Via Nazionale 16, Costa Vopino, T035-971483, navigazionelagoiseo.it. Jun-Sep mainly, services outside this period limited to local needs only.* The government-operated water transport service for Lake Iseo offers fairly regular boats between Iseo and a handful of lakeside towns. They also offer several tourist cruises with guides, including the full day Sebino's Cruise (Jul-Aug, one cruise, Wed and Fri only, €15) which does a full circuit of the lake, Three Islands Tour (Jun-Aug, Sun only, €5.50), a night cruise (Jun-Aug, Fri and Sat only, €35) and special themed excursions, including Franciacorta wine-tastings, and tasting dinners with local products.

Northern and eastern Lake Garda

With its reliable winds, which locals swear breeze in like clockwork, the northern end of Lake Garda is the favoured destination of windsurfers, sailors, and other watersports enthusiasts. Its villages and towns may not be as attractive or refined as elsewhere in the lakes, but the mountains are still very striking, so if getting on the water is your priority, this is the place to head. Popular with Italian families on camping and caravanning holidays, and northern European package tourists on a budget, the eastern side of Garda may not be pretty but there's still plenty of opportunities for swimming and paddling on its shores.

Northern Lake Garda → *For listings, see pages 65-66.*

While fragrant **Limone sul Garda** is set among citrus groves and was a centre for lemon growing until the 1920s, locals claim its name comes from the Latin *limen* (frontier), as it was once a Roman border outpost. It's now Lombardy's last town – Trentino's border is close by – and while it boasts a stunning location on a slim strip of land beneath colossal rocky mountains, its streets have been given over to tourism of the ugliest kind. You'd do well to stay away except during the first days of the season (March) before the shopkeepers have wheeled out their clothes racks of cheap jeans and shelves of tourist tat. Just as dramatically sited at the foot of jagged mountains, **Riva del Garda** is also touristy, but its reliable winds and beaches bring in athletic holidaymakers who settle in for a summer of watersports, somehow making Riva's brand of tourism slightly more palatable. If you're not here for the windsurfing and sailing (most of which happens at nearby **Torbole**), once you've explored the walled *centro storico* and promenaded around the attractive medieval piazza III Novembre, you'll find the rest of Riva dreary with very little to do. Once part of Austria, Riva is more Teutonic culturally, German is widely spoken, most tourists are German (and British), and many Germans and Austrians have holiday homes here, so it might not suit tourists looking for the quintessential Italian Lakes experience.

Eastern Lake Garda → *For listings, see pages 65-66.*

Located in the Verona province of the Veneto region, Lake Garda's eastern shore has an altogether different atmosphere and little of the western shore's allure, with much of the lakefront lined with ugly resorts and dreary-looking camping and caravan parks. While **Malcesine** has a pleasant *centro storico*, the popular windsurfing spot is overrun with package tourists, having totally given over to tourism. **Torri del Benaco** is the most appealing spot, with a tiny but delightful historic core, a picturesque waterfront lined with citrus trees which buzzes during the summer evening's see-and-be-seen stroll, the *passeggiata*, and some ruined towers and battlements remaining from its 10th century walls. Nearby, **Punta San Vigilio** boasts pretty pebble beaches at a lido backed by cypress

Lake Garda's winds

Lake Garda's regular sailors and windsurfers swear you can set your watch by these winds:

Pelèr This gentle breeze (also known as the Vento or Suer) starts around 0200-0300, comes in waves, and lasts until 1100; blowing from the north it brings cool air and clear blue skies to the lake.

Ora Felt mainly in the lake's northern and central parts, this southerly wind picks up where the Pelèr leaves off, around 1200-1300, lasting until sunset; if blowing in the south during summer, it creates cloud on the mountaintops.

Ponale A small, chilly wind from the Valle di Ledro.

Ander A small gust blowing from Desenzano across to Garda.

Vent da Mût A blustery wind following storms.

Vinezza A southerly wind blowing from Peschiera to Maderno; in the late afternoon it's a sign bad weather's on its way.

Balì This turbulent 24-hour wind blows south in winter after snowfalls, creating a choppy lake.

and pine trees, **Parco Baia delle Sirene** ⓘ *Mermaid's Bay Park, T39045-725 5884, Apr-Sep, times and prices vary throughout the season.* Further south, the former fishing village of **Garda** is the only other attractive town this side of the lake, with a little warren of lanes worth exploring in its *centro storico* and a beautiful waterfront promenade with cafés and gelaterias to rival that of Como.

Northern and eastern Lake Garda listings

For hotel and restaurant price codes and other relevant information, see pages 11-14.

🛏 Where to stay

Apart from the charming villages of Torri del Benaco and Garda, the towns of the eastern shore from Riva del Garda to Sirmione are fairly characterless, inundated with package tourists.

Riva del Garda *p64, map p54*
€ Hotel Bellariva, *Via Franz Kafka 13, T0464-553620, hotelbellariva.com.* This three-star is a good-value option for those taking advantage of the nearby sailing and windsurfing opportunities. The 30 rooms are good value and their restaurant does decent pizzas.

Torri del Benaco *p64, map p54*
€€ Hotel Ristorante Gardesana, *Piazza Calderini 20, T0457-225411, hotel-gardesana. com.* An elegant three-star across the road from the small harbour, the 34 rooms are furnished in a 19th-century Venetian style, with modern air conditioning and Wi-Fi. Book one with balcony. Breakfast is excellent, as is their well-regarded restaurant.
€ Garni Onda, *Via per Albisano 28, T0457-225895, garnionda.com.* This little family-run budget B&B-style place is a 100-m walk from the centre and a short stroll to the water. The spacious rooms are sparse but spotless and breakfast is good, as is the service.

Garda *p65, map p54*
€ Albergo Ancora, *Via Manzoni 7, T0457-255202, allancora.com.* While there are

plenty of package resorts and holiday parks around here with handy access to the theme parks, this family-run two-star has far more character. Many of the rooms have lake views, some with balcony or terrace. There's private parking and a bar-restaurant overlooking the lake.

🍴 Restaurants

Riva del Garda *p64, map p54*
€€€ Al Volt, *Via Fiume 73, T0464-552570, ristorantealvolt.com*. A tastefully decorated old restaurant in the historic centre, Al Volt specialises in creative cuisine based on the cooking from Trentino. Try the homemade pasta or the local fish dishes. Sweet-toothed patrons should make sure to peruse the dessert menu, which is filled with classics.

€€ Bella Napoli, *Via de Fabbri 34, T0464-552139*. Wood-fired pizzas are the order of the day here. They appear to come out of the oven every 30 seconds and are just as quickly devoured by hungry locals and visitors who have worked up an appetite sailing and surfing on the lake.

Torri del Benaco *p64, map p54*
€€€ Hotel Ristorante Gardesana, *Piazza Calderini 20, T0457-225411, hotel-gardesana.com*. This establishment really has everything covered with a refined ristorante in the hotel, as well as a smart pizzeria and café. The restaurant has wonderful views from the balcony and refined local cuisine on the menu as well as a smattering of international dishes on offer.

Outdoor activities on Lake Garda

Lake Garda is the home of watersports for the northern Italian lakes and the waters teem with vessels of all kinds during the warmer spring and summer months. Mountain biking, climbing and paragliding are also popular here, and all the sports afford spectacular vistas along with the crisp fresh air of the lake.

Sailing

The lake has some of the best conditions for all forms of sailing in Europe, with a regular breeze arriving nearly every afternoon due to the land around the lake heating up during the day and creating a thermal breeze that funnels through the lake in the afternoon, directed by the mountains either side of the lake. This breeze is called the 'Ora' and in the early morning another breeze often blows, the 'Pelér' or 'Vento', which goes in the opposite direction (north to south). The 'Ora' can measure 4–5 on the Beaufort scale and the 'Pelér' 6–7, but the early surfer or sailor gets the best winds! For full details of the lake's winds, see page 65.

Riva del Garda, or simply Riva to the locals, is sailing central, with almost every type of vessel with a sail found here and dozens of sailing clubs dotted around the pretty shoreline. Further down the lake, where the winds are less heavy, Malcesine is also a popular spot for sailing, as is Sirmione, but none can beat Riva for the breeze. There are plenty of opportunities to rent a *barca a vela* (sailing boat) and take some lessons. One highly recommended centre, **Sailing du Lac** by **Surf Segnana** ① *T0464-552453, sailingdulac.com*, has both catamarans and dinghy-based sailing vessels. For something larger, try **Garda See Charter** ① *T335-527 4554, gscharter.com*, which has yachts as well as smaller vessels, and offers tuition alongside rental and charter. For swapping stories and having a beer after a hard day on the water, head to **Fraglia Vela Riva** ① *via Giancarlo Maroni 2, T0464-552460, fragliavelariva.it*, where most of the area's regattas are headquartered.

Windsurfing

The main centre for windsurfing is Torbole, around the north end of the lake from Riva. Torbole held the RSX world championships in 2006. The best places to head here are **Circolo Surf Torbole** ① *T0464-505385, circolosurftorbole.com*, as well as **Vasco Renna** ① *T0464-505993*, where you can rent a full rig for around €45 a day. **Surf Segnana** ① *T0464-505963, surfsegnana.it*, whose main centre is at Lido di Torbole, offers courses, regardless of level, and children are well catered for if they want to start surfing. All the centres mentioned have excellent and up-to-date equipment. The area is very safe too, as powered leisure craft activities such as water-skiing and jet-skiing are not allowed. If the winds are too much up here, then head down to Malcesine and see the guys at **Stickl** ① *T045-740 1697, stickl.com*, who have been operating here since 1976.

Kitesurfing

Kitesurfers are increasingly finding Lake Garda a great place for kiting even if landing and launching can feel a little daunting with those tall trees and sheer cliffs all around. Campione del Garda is a very popular place to kite surf and has an association there, **Kite Surf Campione** ① *kitecampione.it*, while for lessons it's best to head to **Kite School Xkite** ① *T338-828 7886, xkite.it*, at Brenzone on the opposite side of the lake.

Paragliding

If you're keen to get even more airtime and want to try paragliding, head to **Arco** ① *Volo Libero Alto Garda, via Ravazzone 87, T0464-910579*, at the head of the lake, or **Malcesine** ① *Paragliding Club Malcesine, via Gardesana 228, T335-611 2902*.

Other activities

If you prefer to stay on the ground, but fancy venturing out with some views of the lake, then perhaps do a spot of mountain biking, climbing or Nordic walking. Mountain bikes can be rented just about anywhere on the lake and the **Visit Garda** website (visitgarda. com) has maps of the many different (and very extensive) paths around the lake. Rock climbers and Nordic walkers head to **Arco**, where it's best to start at **Guide Alpine Arco** ① *via S Caterina 40, T0464-507075, guidealpinearco.com*, where they can give you all the information you need to embark upon mountain activities safely.

Contents

Footprint features

Towns of the Po Valley

Brescia

Brescia is a buzzing little city. Once the Roman city of Brixia, it's now a living and working town with a vibrant centro storico boasting several pedestrian-only shopping thoroughfares and lively interconnecting piazzas that are a delight to wander. It may not be breathtakingly beautiful but it has a handful of architectural gems including an elegant loggia, an old and 'new' Duomo, a splendid Broletto, and a Visconti castle. Despite being brilliantly located between Milan and Verona, if you're travelling by train, or between Lakes Como and Garda on a lakes drive, Brescia gets by-passed by most travellers. A centre for industry and commerce – although that's only visible on the drive in from the *autostrada* – Brescia is home to a multicultural population of immigrant workers from Asia, Africa and the Middle East. It's this grittily authentic, ethno-Italian vibe and lack of tourists that make Brescia so appealing, and a visit here so refreshing.

Brescia's piazzas

Piazza della Vittoria is as fine a piazza as any from which to begin to explore, and starting here makes sense if you have a car, as there's a public car park. The piazza is surrounded by striking, colossal structures of the movement known as *Novecento* (meaning 1900s, but closely associated with the Fascist era). Designed by Marcello Piacentini, the architect responsible for Rome's impressive EUR district, it's a must-do for architecture and design buffs; note the marble-striped post office and the very cool off-centre clock on the white marble tower.

From here, head north on via Post to the 15th-century **piazza Loggia**, Brescia's most attractive square. It's home to the enormous elegant Venetian Renaissance **Palazzo della Loggia**, a lovely place to cool off on a sultry summer's day. Spot the Roman stones embedded into the building on the square's southern side, where the tourist office is. The **Torre dell'Orologio** was inspired by Venice's campanile in piazza San Marco and below the clock tower you'll note a memorial to eight people killed and a hundred-odd injured here in the 1974 Fascist bombing of a trade union rally. You should also be able to see some damage to the pillar near where the bomb was left in a rubbish bin.

The tiny lanes immediately north of piazza della Loggia are interesting and worth a look. If you're staying here for a couple of days then explore the area north of here, which is home to Brescia's immigrant population. While a little rough round the edges (some may even find it intimidating), it's safe: corso Mameli is crammed with shops, delis, cafés and bars and there's a cheap clothes market on piazza Rovetta, while contrada del Carmine is the city's old red light district.

Back on piazza della Loggia, take the bustling passage immediately east, via Dieci Giornate (note the delicatessens under the arcades), to **piazza Papa Paolo VI**, formerly piazza del Duomo. Alternatively, you can take the slightly longer and more interesting way around to the piazza through the medieval tower-gate **Porta Bruciata**, in the northeast corner of the square, to **via del Musei**, an atmospheric street. There are several restaurants full of character here and along **via Beccaria**, which leads down to piazza Papa Paolo VI, and there are good cafés and eateries on and around piazzetta Tito Speri.

Piazza Papa Paolo VI, named after the Brescian-born Pope Paul VI (1897-1978), is a picturesque square that's presided over by the splendid 13th-century **Broletto**, still a working administrative centre, with a wonderful courtyard that's worth wandering into to admire its carved reliefs and frescoes. Exit on the opposite side of the Broletto and turn left onto via Mazzini to meet back up with via dei Musei to take in **Roman Brixia** (see page 73), and on the hill overlooking it, the **Castello**. Or, return to piazza Papa Paolo VI to visit the Duomos.

Duomo Nuovo

ⓘ *Piazza Papa Paolo VI, T030-42714. Mon-Sat 0730-1200 and 1600-1930, Sun 0800-1300 and 1600-1930, free.*

Rather unusually for Italian towns where a new church is normally built upon an old one, or reconstructed using materials of the former, the enormous Duomo Nuovo (new cathedral) and squat Duomo Vecchio (old cathedral) sit side by side. The old church is dwarfed by the imposing 'new' 17th-century cathedral, which took 200 years to build – which many locals argue was 200 years too long. The exterior has a restrained Renaissance

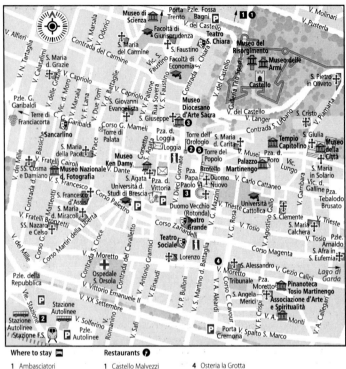

Where to stay 🛏

1 Ambasciatori
2 NH Brescia
3 Vittoria

Restaurants 🍴

1 Castello Malvezzi
2 Locanda dei Guasconi
3 Osteria al Bianchi
4 Osteria la Grotta
5 Vasco da Gama

façade with minimal ornamentation other than some elegant statues and carvings, while the interior hosts the tomb of Sant'Apollonio, notable paintings and sculptures, and an enormous 80-m high 19th-century cupola, the third largest in Italy.

Duomo Vecchio

ⓘ *Piazza Papa Paolo VI, T030-42714. Tue-Sun 0900-1200 and 1600-1900, free.*

Many find the old cathedral, also called the Rotonda, far more intriguing than its neighbour. As it's sunk slightly below piazza level, the fine Romanesque structure and features of the circular 11th-century church aren't easily appreciated. Built on top of an early Christian basilica, which in turn was established upon Roman baths (preserved beneath glass inside), it houses fine medieval paintings and the 13th-century red-marble tomb of Berardo Maggi, Bishop of Brescia. The level you enter at was the *matroneum*, a prayer gallery reserved for women. Dress code is strictly adhered to, so dress modestly.

A walking tour of Roman Brixia

Remains of the important Roman city of Brixia, designated *Colonia Civica Augusta* in 27 BC, are still in evidence in Brescia today:

Decumanus maximus You can begin a walk along the ancient main east-west street, which is now via dei Musei, beginning from the Broletto.

Roman Forum Piazza del Foro was built over the ancient centre of Brixia, thought to have been much larger in its day.

Tempio Capitolino The towering marble columns of the *Capitolium*, a partly reconstructed Roman temple, built in AD 73 by Emperor Vespasian, still stand and can be visited (via Musei 55, T030-297 7834, Tue-Sun 1000-1300 and 1400-1700, free) the brick parts are from the reconstruction in 1939.

Teatro Romano Frescoes from an older temple have been found at this partly excavated Roman amphitheatre just past *Tempio Capitolino* on the left.

Mosaic floors from Roman villas Well-preserved mosaics are on display in the **Museo della Città** (Museo di Santa Giulia, via Musei, Tue-Sun 1000-1800, €8), along with other archaeological finds from Brixia.

Il Castello

ⓘ *Cidneo Hill, via del Castello 9, T030-293292. Oct-May Tue-Sun 0930-1700, Jun-Sep Tue-Sun 1000-1800, museum prices start at €5.*

Overlooking the remains of Roman Brixia, and once an early Roman site itself written about by the ancient poet Catullus (and before that a Bronze Age settlement), the 14th-century Visconti castle is accessed from via dei Musei past a lane that winds up to the wooded Cydnean Hill. Adapted by the Venetians, French and Austrians, the fortress' myriad drawbridges, ramparts, towers and courtyards are a mishmash of military styles with its most impressive structure being an imposing keep with a 22-m high cylindrical tower, dating to the 13th century, known as the 'Mirabella'. While the castle's labyrinth of rooms and passages house several small decent museums dedicated to weaponry, astronomy and the Italian Risorgimento, the best thing to do is simply enjoy the views and picnic in the surrounding forested parkland.

Brescia listings

For hotel and restaurant price codes and other relevant information, see pages 11-14.

🛏 Where to stay

Brescia *p70, map p72*

€€€ Hotel Vittoria, *Via X Giornate 20, T030-280061, hotelvittoria.com.* The only real choice in the historic centre, but thankfully it's an admirable one, with a handsome exterior and an elegant neoclassical interior. The rooms are in very good condition and the suites are enormous; all are well-equipped, including fast internet.

€€ Hotel Ambasciatori, *Via S Crocifissa Di Rosa 92, T030-399114, ambasciatori.net.* Located just outside the historic centre (about a 10-minute walk), this hotel is popular with business travellers and the rooms and friendly service make up for the rather mundane exterior. A small gym and Wi-Fi keeps guests happy as does the better than average breakfast offerings.

€€ NH Brescia, *Viale Stazione 15, T030-44221, nh-hotels.it.* This modern four-star hotel, part of the Spanish NH chain, is typical of their style of hotel, being contemporary with good attention to detail and an excellent level of service and amenities. The hotel is around 10 minutes walk from the historic centre and has a good restaurant and bar.

Restaurants

Brescia *p70, map p72*

€€€€ Ristorante Castello Malvezzi, *Via Colle S Giuseppe 1, T030-200 4224, castellomalvezzi.it.* It's not often that you get to dine on the terrace of a 16th-century hunting lodge, and it's more of a castle really. Expect creative, refined local cuisine and considerate service.

€€ Locanda Dei Guasconi, *Via C Beccaria 11, T030-377 1605, locandadeiguasconi. it.* Down this busy 'eat street' Locanda Dei Guasconi has a cosy rustic Italian interior but a glassed-in 'outside' dining area reminiscent of a classic French bistro. The food, however, is very Brescian. Expect plenty of polenta dishes (try the wild boar stew if it's on the menu) and excellent local wines.

€€ Osteria Al Bianchi, *Via Gasparo da Salò 32, T030-292328, osteriaalbianchi.it.* This simple, no-nonsense osteria in the heart of the old centre serves up honest, hearty fare. Try their spinach and ricotta dumplings or, for the more brave, their *brasato d'asino* (braised donkey), a rustic local speciality. Being an osteria the wines are excellent too.

€€ Vasco Da Gama, *Via Musei 4 (alternative entrance on via Beccaria), T030-375 4039.* A restaurant brimming with character, this has rustic charm but also a more modern, glassed-in area overlooking via Beccaria.

The cuisine is unapologetically Brescian with that hearty, no-compromise style and laden with the well-loved local butter.

€ Osteria La Grotta, *Vicolo del Prezzemelo 10, T030-44068, osterialagrotta.it.* One of the oldest in town, it's also one of the most endearing, with frescoes on the walls, well-worn wooden furniture, and hams hanging from the ceiling. Clearly their hams are excellent, as are the cheeses, and there are some cherished local dishes that are hard to find in many restaurants such as *trippa in brodo* – tripe in consommé.

Entertainment

Brescia *p70, map p72*
Bars and clubs

There are lots of bars between piazza della Loggia and piazza Paolo and the surrounding streets in the *centro storico* that start to hot up around aperitivo time and stay open late, especially at weekends. Also popular for aperitivo is the piazzale Arnaldo area which boasts views over the countryside.

Caffè Duomo Pasticceria, *opposite Duomo Vecchio.* The alfresco tables on the piazza are a lovely place for a quiet afternoon drink.

Muse e Musei, *Piazza Brusato 24, T030-45048. Thu-Tue until 0200.* This popular jazz club gets crowded late at night with local students and musos piling in and sinking in to the sofas to listen to live music.

Osteria Al Bianchi, *Via Gasparo de Salò 42, T030-292328. Thu-Mon.* This is one of the most popular bars for a drink in this busy area; great wines by the glass, with good local options.

Osteria Vecchio Botticino, *Piazzale Arnaldo 6, T030-48103. Mon-Sat until 0100.* Just east of the old centre, this cool low-lit bar attracts locals who like to sit with a glass of wine for a while as they take in the scene.

Classical music, opera and theatre

Brescia is home to the Brixia Symphony Orchestra with a woman conductor –

Giovanna Sorbi. She's also the Artistic director of the Festival di Musica Sacra (Sacred Music Festival), held in various churches in the city from February through to June. Check the Comune di Brescia website (comune.brescia.it) for details or visit the tourist office.

O Shopping

Brescia *p70, map p72*
Brescia has a lively and fascinating shopping scene, which should be no surprise considering it's a centre for industry and manufacturing with a large immigrant population. The best shopping is on and around corsos Zanardelli and Magenta in the centre of the old town, and between there and piazza Vittoria and piazza Loggia.

Clothing and accessories
Interno 5, *Contrada Cavaletto 5, T030-375 7436.* One for the guys, this cool store stocks casual men's clothes. Expect anything from printed Commes des Garcons t-shirts to Ugo Cacciatori's baroque-meets-Damien Hirst jewellery.
Penelope, *Via A Gramsci 16/A, T03-46902, penelopestores.com.* One of Italy's most eclectically- and adventurously-curated women's fashion stores stocking clothes, shoes and accessories labels that err on the audacious side, including Azzedine Alaia, Martin Margiela, and Sigourney.

Food and drink
Piazza del Mercato is home to a bustling food market. In the darkness under the porticos there are dozens of delicatessens. If you're looking for an *alimentari, salumeria, panetteria, pasticceria* or *enoteca*, so you can stock up on those picnic supplies, this is where to find it!

O What to do

Brescia *p70, map p72*
Cycling
Brescia has a free bike-borrowing scheme during summer. Bikes can be collected and returned from outside the main train station (0730-1930) but visit the tourist office (piazza Loggia 6, T030-240 0357, comune.brescia.it) for cycling route suggestions.

Food and wine
The **Associazione Strada del Vino Franciacorta** (via Verdi 53, Erbusco, near Brescia, T307-760870, stradadelfranciacorta.it) organizes a range of activities in the Franciacorta wine region near Brescia, including the wine-focused Festival del Franciacorta, dozens of wine events, cellar-door tasting and vineyard tours throughout the year. They also offer themed walking, cycling, and horseriding tours and can arrange tailor-made excursions to wineries.

Cremona

Compact Cremona is one of the region's most compelling towns. There is no denying that most visitors are drawn here for the little city's fascinating history of violin-making, to appreciate the fine craftsmanship of the masters, the Amati family, and the most famous craftsman of all, Antonio Stradivari, whose violins are the most valuable musical instruments on the planet. But what makes Cremona such a delight to visit is that the violins and violas are not just museum pieces in the city, although there is certainly plenty of polished wood around to admire. Dozens of instrument-makers toil away in workshops dotted around the town to this day, hand-making instruments to a meticulous tradition. The beautiful sound of the instruments being played frequently fills the air, lending Cremona a tone of refinement and sophistication not found in many places.

Piazza del Comune

This splendid town might be most famous as the home of violin-making, but it's worth visiting for its stunning architecture alone, most of which is on the main square. The enormous **piazza del Comune** is one of northern Italy's most elegant squares with its breezy arcades, charming loggias and alfresco cafes, and the monumental 12th-century **Cattedrale di Santa Maria Assunta** as its centrepiece. Adjoining the cathedral is the colossal **Torrazzo**, one of the tallest bell towers in Italy (you'll notice it from the *autostrade*), and on the other side of the church, a charming octagonal **Baptistery**, tiny in comparison. There's a crenellated city hall, the **Palazzo Comunale**, and the rather handsome red-brick **Loggia dei Militi**, all of which make a stroll around the square something of an architectural tour in itself.

The piazza del Comune may be where your sightseeing starts but the piazza and its surrounding streets are also the centre of the city's social life and where you'll find yourself hanging out after dark. The streets of Cremona are alive with young music students and aspiring violin-makers who flock here from all around the world to learn the craft and, in summer when school's out, the students cram the squares in the evenings with beers in hand and the city really buzzes. Cremona's families and older folk pull up chairs at the alfresco cafés on the square or simply wander about with gelatos, giving the city a laid-back atmosphere that's addictive. Prepare yourself for staying longer than you planned.

Cattedrale di Santa Maria Assunta

① *Piazza del Comune, T035-383 2411. Mon-Sat 1030-1200 and 1530-1800, Sun 1030-1100 and 1530-1730, free.*

While the size of Cremona's enormous red-brick Duomo, the Cattedrale di Santa Maria Assunta, dating to 1107, is what initially impresses most – it's truly colossal and it does take time to take it all in – the detail is stunning too. A superb example of Lombard Romanesque church architecture, its splendid marble façade boasts a beautiful rose window, pretty rows of open galleries, and a portal crowned with statues within niches. Inside there is a brick apse and transepts, but it's the vivid 16th-century frescoes of Mary and Jesus that capture attention. Back outside, an elegant, red-tile-roofed, Renaissance marble loggia, known as 'La Bertazzola', takes you from the cathedral to the lofty **Torrazzo** ① *Tue-Sun 1000-1300, summer 1530-1730, €5*, which at 111 m remains one of the country's tallest medieval bell towers and clock towers, and has magnificent vistas of the town. There is little to see – apart from columns and high balconies – inside the brick interior of the nearby **Baptistery**, dating to 1167, and you are better off heading to the museums.

Collezione Gli Archi in Sala dei Violini

① *Palazzo Comunale, piazza del Comune 8, T0372-20502. Tue-Sat 0900-1800, Sun 1000-1800, €6.60, combined ticket including Museo Civica Ala Ponzone €10.*

Located at the top of a sweeping staircase in the lavish Palazzo Comunale building in the *Sala dei Violini* (violin room), opposite the cathedral, this small but exquisite collection of musical instruments should send musicians' hearts racing. Perhaps the most prominent pieces of the collection – ones that even those who aren't fans or musicians would want to see – are the instruments crafted by Antonio Stradivari. The

Historical city itineraries

Pick up a detailed city map from Cremona's excellent tourist office (piazza del Comune 5, T0372-23233, aptcremona. it) before setting out to discover these architectural gems from different ages:

The Roman and Early Middle Ages City

Stroll along via Solferino (the ancient Roman *cardus minor*, or side street), then via Capra Plasio (for the Roman mosaics), before visiting the archaeological section of the Museo Civico Ala Ponzone. Finish with the former Basilica of San Lorenzo and Chiesa di San Michele Vetere.

The Medieval City

Start on the main piazza with visits to the Cathedral, Torrazzo, Baptistery, Loggia di Militi, Town Hall, Cittanova Palace, then the Chiesa di Sant'Agata and Chiesa di Sant'Agostino.

The Renaissance City

Enjoy the city's many stunning Renaissance churches, including San Sigismondo, Santa Margherita, San Pietro di Po, and Sant'Abbondio, as well as Raimondi Palace and Affaitati Palace.

The 18th-Century City

Visit the splendid churches of San Vincenzo, Sant'Ilario and Sant'Omobono, before checking out the elegant Stanga-Rossi San Secondo, Silva-Persichelli and Mina-Bolzesi *palazzi*, and the Ponchielli theatre.

City of Violins

Start with the Stradivari Museum and the Collezione Gli Archi in Sala dei Violini. You could also visit Stradivari's house (corso Garibaldi 57) and grave (in the public gardens), the International School of Violin Making, and the Fodri and Pallavicino *palazzi*.

surviving instruments of Stradivari are so renowned that they all have 'names' that are often based on famous ex-owners.

The large format *Il Cremonese* is one of only 10 instruments crafted by Stradivari in 1715 during his golden period. The instruments made in this year are amongst his most coveted creations. *Il Cremonese* was once owned by famous violinist and composer of the 19th century, Joseph Joachim, so is sometimes referred to as the *ex-Joachim* Stradivarius.

A second violin, the *Vesuvius*, dates from 1727 when the master was in his most mature period as a violin-maker. Bequeathed to the museum by English violinist and composer Remo Lauricella, it was named *Vesuvius* after its original bright red varnish. The colour of the instrument has turned brown over the years, the apparent result of heat and humidity from a stint in India.

In contrast to these two instruments of the mature Stradivari, a violin of his from 1669, *Il Clisbee*, shows the clear influence of Nicolò Amati, of whom Stradivari was a pupil. Herbert Axelrod, a famous philanthropist and collector of classical instruments, donated the instrument to the museum in 2003.

Another fascinating instrument is Stradivari's violincello, *Cristiani*, dating to 1700, which was the master's attempt at making a smaller cello. This was one of only two examples of violincellos from this year that are in existence. Note the fine maple wood used by Stradivari and its rich plum-red varnish.

Another instrument of interest is Nicolò Amati's 1658 violin, *L'Hammerle*. This is a classic example of just what fine instruments Stradivari's mentor was capable of, with beautiful workmanship and still some of the original varnish intact.

Museo Civico Ala Ponzone

① *Palazzo Affaitati, via Ugolani Dati 4, T0372-407269. Tue-Sat 0900-1800, Sun 1000-1800, €7, combined ticket including Collezione Gli Archi in Sala dei Violini €11.*

The Museo Civico Ala Ponzone is really three museums in one building: the Sezione Archeologica, the Pinacoteca and the Museo Stradivariano. The compact archaeological section contains exhibits of Egyptian treasures (the amulets are beautiful), ancient Greek finds (the vases and urns are a real highlight), and Roman relics (the glassware is pretty); however, the Pinacoteca (picture gallery), which you can view on your way to the Museo Stradivariano, is of more interest, with works by Caravaggio, Cremonese artists, and notable collections of porcelain, ceramics and ivory.

The *Museo Stradivariano* is what most people come to see. This wonderful collection was started in 1893 after a collection of moulds, patterns and tools of some of the greatest violin-makers, including Antonio Stradivari, were donated to the town of Cremona. The most significant part of the museum is from the collection of Ignazio Alessandro Cozio who had purchased part of the workshop of Stradivari. The museum is in three parts, the first being based around the construction of a contralto viola in the traditional Cremonese manner. The second part is comprised of instruments from violin-makers of the second half of the 19th century and the first half of the 20th century. Finally, the Salabue-Fiorini collection comprises 16 cases containing 710 fascinating artefacts from the workshop of Antonio Stradivari. While the museum is engaging for anyone interested in classical music, woodwork or instrument-making, it might only be a quick visit for others, albeit an insightful one.

Cremona listings

For hotel and restaurant price codes and other relevant information, see pages 11-14.

● Where to stay

Cremona *p76*
The tourist office (piazza del Comune, T0372-23233) has a long list of B&Bs and *agriturismo* properties on their books, ranging from simple and sparse, to rustic and cosy. The helpful staff can arrange accommodation for you. Most are in the countryside outside Bergamo, so you'll require transport.

€€ Dellearti Design Hotel, *Via Bonomelli 8, T0372-23131, dellearti.com*. The 'design hotel' craze saw some interesting designs as well as some that didn't work or age so well. This hotel tips towards the latter category, with the industrial theme and dim lighting

a little off-putting. The unbeatable location (less than a block from the main square), secure parking, and friendly reception staff more than make up for it. Great discounts off-season.

€€ Hotel Continental, *Piazza della Libertà 26, T0372-434141, hotelcontinentalcremona. it*. This modern hotel is a safe choice, with 62 rooms and a four-star rating. Rooms are comfortable and quiet and it's in an okay location if you don't wish to drive through the historic centre.

● Restaurants

Cremona *p76*
€€€ Il Violino, *Via Sicardo 3 (off piazza Duomo), T037-246 1010, ilviolino.it*. While it's not a very original name for a restaurant in the home of the violin, we'll forgive it as it's such a handsome one. There's plenty of

pasta and risotto dishes – try their house special *risotto con zucca, mostarda ed amaretti* (risotto with pumpkin and local mustard fruits), while main courses are filling meat or fish options. A strong wine list and good service.

€€ La Botte, *Via Porta Marzia 5/a, T037-229640, tavernalabotte.net*. This wonderful old tavern has atmosphere by the barrel load, from the exposed wooden ceiling to the old wine casks transformed into chairs and tables. It has delicious food too, with some wonderful dishes such as *malfatti con funghi porcini* (dumplings with porcini mushrooms), lots of seafood, and plates of cured meats and cheeses.

€€ La Sosta, *Via Vescovo Sicardo 9, T037-245 6656, osterialasosta.it*. Not far from the main plaza, this local favourite is everything a good Italian eatery should be. It has a warm and inviting atmosphere, handmade pasta (try the gnocchi), excellent salami and hams, and local seasonal specialities such as *tartufo freschi d'Alba* (fresh truffles from Alba). Great regional wines and fine service.

€ Centrale, *Vicolo Pertusio 4, T037-228701*. Just as it says, this traditional trattoria is centrally located, and has a firm following for its straightforward fare of regional favourites. Among others, try their *tortelli di zucca* (pasta with pumpkin filling) – it'll require a couple of laps around the main square to work off!

ⓘ Entertainment

Cremona *p76*
Bars and clubs
There are several café-bars on the main squares of piazza del Comune and piazza del Pace, overlooking the colossal Duomo, that are wonderful for a gelato or an aperitivo in the evening. **Portici del Comune** (piazza del Comune 2, T0372-21295), an atmospheric old place tucked under the arcades, is popular with locals, with tables spread right out into the square at night.

Classical music, opera and theatre
Teatro Amilcare Ponchielli, *Corso Vittorio Emanuele 52, T0372-022001, teatroponchielli. it*. This superb theatre hosts the Festival di Cremona every May, along with a full programme of orchestras and concerts, from Gregorian Chant to Byzantine music.

ⓞ Shopping

Cremona *p76*
Il Consorzio Liutai Antonio Stradivari, *Piazza Stradivari 1, T0372-463503, cremonaliuteria.it*. The Consortium of Antonio Stradivari Violinmakers has exquisite handmade violins for sale in their showroom, from €5,000 to €14,000 for a concert-standard instrument. If you're serious about buying a violin and you want to order one, the Consortium is happy to advise and organize a visit to a workshop.

Food and drink
Negozio Sperlari, *Via Solferino 25, T0372-22346, sperlari1836.com*. Visit the historic 'Antica Bottega di Strada Solferino' for gourmet foods (over 3,500 items apparently), including confectionery, nuts, sweet wines, liqueurs, and Cremona's specialty *torrone* (nougat), and you'll see why they were made purveyors to the Royal Family in 1921. Take something home by **Agusto Fieschi** (fieschi1867.com), manufacturers of *mostarda* and *torrone* since 1867. Maximus is the *torrone* to get, reputedly cooked for 10 hours and hand cut. Enjoy it with a bottle of winemaker Beppe Bassi's Sol dessert wine, created from Picolit and Molinelli grapes grown a few kilometres away and produced by the Fregoni family.

ⓞ What to do

Cremona *p76*
Food and wine
Strada Del Gusto Cremonese, *Piazza del Comune 5, T0372-406391, stradadelgustocremonese.it*. The 'Cremonese

Taste Route', the group that promotes Cremona's gastronomic traditions and products, organizes a range of festivals, events, tours and activities held throughout the year.

Sightseeing

Associazione Guide Turistiche ed Interpreti di Cremona, *Piazza Giovanni XXIII, T0372-37970. Summer Mon-Fri 1000-1200, rest of year Mon-Wed 1500-1700, cremonatour.net.* Cremona has its act together when it comes to guides with a top-notch organisation of highly qualified multi-lingual guides offering city walking tours to themed excursions. Groups of six preferred, personalised tours can be arranged.

Walking

The tourist office (see below) produces an excellent brochure and map – *Cremona City of Art and Music: Six Itineraries to Discover the City* – outlining self-guided walks on the following themes: The Roman and early Middle Ages; The Middle Ages; The Renaissance City; The Spanish and the 18th Century; The City and Music; and The City and Po River.

❶ Directory

Cremona *p76*
Money Via Dante, via Manzoni, corso Mazzini. **Medical services** Istituti Ospitalieri Di Cremona, viale Concordia 1, T0372-4051. **Farmacia Leggeri Dr Alberto**, corso Matteotti Giacomo 22, T0372-22210. **Post office** Via Verdi 1, T0372-593551 (Mon-Fri 0830-1900, Sat 0830-1230). **Tourist information** Piazza del Comune 5, T0372-23233, comune.cremona. it (daily 0900-1230, 1500-1800). **Train station** Via Dante, T892021, trenitalia.it.

Mantua

Diminutive Mantova (Mantua is the anglicized version) must be one of the most magnificently located cities in Italy. The walled city dominates its small peninsula, with water on three sides, the Mincio River having been formed into three man-made lakes – Lago Inferiore, Lago di Mezzo and Lago Superiore – in the 12th century, for defensive purposes. The lakes are a blessing and a curse; they provide delicious fresh fish to Mantua's tables all year, but send swarms of mosquitoes through the city during the summer. Like Venice and the other cities of the low Po plains, Mantua gets swelteringly hot in summer. However, when there's a breeze blowing across the lake and into the town's arcades and squares on a balmy evening, there are few more pleasant places to be.

It's hard to imagine how a gorgeous city, dominated by a majestic castle and surrounded by serene lakes, could be a hidden gem, but Mantua is. It's less than 40 km from Lake Garda and 30 km from Verona, yet few visitors include it on their itineraries. Those who drop by on a day trip inevitably wish they'd stayed longer. Mantua's attractions might be obvious – a colossal castle, sumptuous baroque churches, lazy piazzas, and elegant *palazzi* filled with frescoes – yet like Brescia, its real appeal is the distinct lack of tourists (even in high season) and an unassuming elegance. While there's a postcard stand or two outside the old-fashioned *alimentari* (grocery shops) on piazza Sordello, mostly they're inhabited by locals buying bread and a newspaper. The locals ride bikes around the largely pedestrianized streets of the *centro storico* and linger at tables set up on the cobblestones, separated by potted oleander bushes. Like Brescia, Mantua has a sizeable foreign population and it's not unusual to see immigrants lined up at the government offices sorting out their new lives. Yet it's this kind of everyday activity about the city that gives it an authenticity that's hard to find elsewhere. That, combined with the history and beauty, is what makes Mantua so alluring.

Mantua's piazzas

Mantua is a city of handsome squares all interconnecting, making it easy to explore. The spacious cobblestone **piazza Sordello** is Mantua's main square, presided over by the big baroque Duomo at its northern end, the enormous Palazzo Ducale and its lovely arcades and gardens sprawled on the eastern side, and several *palazzi*, including a striking crenellated red-brick façade, on the western side; there are several pleasant alfresco cafés here too. A passageway takes you beneath the brick Broletto and the lofty medieval tower, the Torre della Gabbia, into tiny **piazza Broletto**, which in turn takes you along a laneway lined on both sides by arcades with elegant shops and cafés tucked beneath them to the next square. On **piazza Erbe** you'll find the elegant 13th-century Palazzo della Ragione (with wonderful frescoes inside in the upper chamber) and a beautiful 15th-century **Torre dell'Orologio** (clock tower) with a golden zodiac on its inner 'dial' and faded frescoes on the outer circle. There are several good restaurants under the arcades that neatly spread their tables out on the piazza in warmer weather, while on Thursday mornings there's a busy market here. The piazza is also home to the Rotonda San Lorenzo (see page 84); opposite is the tourist office. Piazza Erbe joins tiny **piazza Mantegna**, which is dominated by the enormous **Basilica di Sant'Andrea**, which in turn leads down a lovely cobblestone street lined with pavement cafés and smart shops to **piazza Marconi**, and then onto corso Umberto and the busy transport hub (the taxi stand is here) of **piazza Cavallotti**, where you'll find the neoclassical **Teatro Sociale**.

Castello di San Giorgio and Palazzo Ducale

ⓘ *Piazza Sordello, T037-224832, mantovaducale.beniculturali.it. Tue-Sun 0815-1915 (last tickets 1830), €6.50.*

Mantua's main attraction is its monumental castle, which is the only thing many visitors to the city see. It's actually a complex of several majestic buildings, including the Castello di San Giorgio, and the Palazzo Ducale, which were seized from the ruling Bonacolsi in 1328 by Luigi Gonzaga, at the start of the dynasty's 300-year period of rule. Once Europe's largest royal residence, at the height of its power over a thousand people lived and worked here in its 500 rooms, and when the Austrians looted the place in 1630 it's said they used 80 carriages to cart off all the riches including 2,000 paintings. While the complex is crammed with room after room of Renaissance treasures, most people make a beeline for the brilliantly restored frescoes of the Gonzaga family painted by Andrea Mantegna from 1465-1474 in the Camera degli Sposi ('the bedroom of the wedded couple'). The frescoes are stunning. Considered one of Mantegna's greatest works, they contain all the attributes that made the artist great, from the three-dimensional quality to the exquisite attention to detail. Keep in mind it could easily take you a couple of hours to get there if you stop and spend time in each of the splendid rooms on your way. There are around 40 rooms to see, and if you're a fan of castles you could easily spend the good part of a day here. During winter, when there are few visitors, you're required to do a guided tour (times posted outside), but the rest of the year you have a choice between doing a guided tour, self-guided visit, or an audio guide. Numbers are restricted to 20 people at 10-minute intervals for the Camera degli Sposi, so book ahead if visiting during the peak spring and autumn periods. Also worth viewing are the splendid frescoed summer rooms of Isabella d'Este, which can be seen by anyone but only by appointment on weekends.

Duomo

ⓘ *Piazza Sordello, T0376-320220. Daily 0700-1200 & 1500-1900, free.*
The piazza's other outstanding monument is the striking 14th-century Duomo, also known as the Cattedrale San Pietro. Even travellers who have been in Italy a while and are bored with churches inevitably find themselves drawn inside this intriguing Duomo, eager to see what the interior of such an unusual cathedral might look like. The red-brick Romanesque exterior has minaret-like towers and an austere white late-baroque façade with restrained ornamentation and statues of saints on top, while the interior is richly decorated with fluted columns that hold up elaborately gilded ceilings and a beautiful frescoed cupola.

Rotonda San Lorenzo

ⓘ *Piazza Erbe, T0376-320220. Daily 1000-1200 and 1430-1630, donations welcome.*
The city's oldest church, dating to 1082, was presumed to have been 'lost' until the little round red-brick structure was re-discovered in 1908 when the buildings surrounding it were destroyed. Like the Duomo Vecchio in Brescia, it is sunken beneath piazza level, has bare brick walls, and there is a separate women's prayer gallery. There are also some lovely faded medieval frescoes.

Palazzo Te

ⓘ *Viale Te, T0376-323266. Mon 1300-1800 and Tue-Sun 0900-1800, €8.*
This sumptuous Renaissance-Mannerist palazzo was designed by the celebrated architect-artist Giulio Romano (who spent 10 years from 1525-1535 decorating it). It was built for Federico Gonzaga II as a romantic retreat and pleasure dome to enjoy with his lover Isabella – which explains the exuberant decor and erotic frescoes featuring scenes of bacchanalian excess. It just goes to show what's possible when artistic imaginations are allowed to run wild!

Mantua listings

For hotel and restaurant price codes and other relevant information, see pages 11-14.

⬤ Where to stay

Mantua *p82*
Mantua has a consortium, **Agriturismo Mantua** (Largo Porta Pradella 1, T0376-324889, agriturismomantova.it) that features a wide selection of agriturismo accommodation; as most are in the countryside, you'll need a car to get there and get around.

€€ Albergo Bianchi Stazione, *Piazza Don E Leoni 24, T0376-326465, albergobianchi.com.* A welcoming, friendly and family-run hotel across from the train station and a 10-minute stroll from the historic centre, some of the 53 well-kept rooms overlook the hotel's private garden.
€ Armellino B&B, *Via Cavour 67, T346-314 8060, bebarmellino.it.* This modish B&B is right in the heart of the old town, set in an 18th-century palace with a lovely blend of antique and contemporary touches. There

are only three rooms, two standard rooms and a larger suite, and all are excellent value – but cash only.

€ Corte San Girolamo, *Strada San Girolamo 1*, *T347-8008505* , *agriturismo-sangirolamo. it*. Located 3 km from the old town, this *agriturismo* estate has 14 simply decorated rooms in rustic style with exposed wooden beam ceilings and tiled floors. There is plenty of wildlife to spot and the place has bicycles that you can use to ride the 40 km of tracks around the region.

€ Hotel Broletto ,*Via Accademia 1*, *T037-632 6784, hotelbroletto.com*. A great location is the prime attraction of this small but somewhat dated hotel but it's quite cosy all the same.

❼ Restaurants

Mantua *p82*

€€€€ Aquila Nigra, *Vicolo Bonacolsi 4*, *T0376-327180, aquilanigra.it*. This former convent near the Palazzo Ducale is still a place of virtue and worship, but it's now about the delightful rendering of Mantua's best dishes. The *saltarelli e frittata di zucchine* (freshwater shrimps with zucchini) is a must, but try their greatest hits with the degustation menu. They also have a more casual osteria next door, La Porta Accanto, but be sure to book ahead for the restaurant.

€€ Fragoletta Antica, *Piazza Arche 5a*, *T0376-323300, fragoletta.it*. One of the oldest osterias in town, it serves up local classics with a modern sense of style and presentation. Try the tortelli filled with pumpkin.

€ Grifone Bianco, *Piazza dell'Erbe 6*, *T0376-365423, grifonebianco.it*. If you're wandering around this lovely square trying to decide where to eat, this is the place to head – great local salami, scrumptious risotto, and handmade *gnocchetti* (small dumplings), and it's all good value too.

€ Ochina Bianca, *Via Finzi 2, T0376-323700, ochinabianca.it*. This osteria is elegant, while being cosy and inviting. Also inviting is the menu, packed full of local specialities but updated with flair. Try their signature slow-cooked donkey dish, *stracotto d'asino al lambrusco con polenta*.

Around Mantua

The area around Mantua is famous for its cuisine. One of the first complete cookbooks, *L'Arte di Ben Cucinare* was penned here by Bartolomeo Stefani in 1662. While others had published recipes, Stefani included 'ordinary' dishes, not just those served at fancy banquets. Today the region is just as influential as there are many highly regarded restaurants in the area around Mantua – led by the trio featured below. Remember to book ahead.

€€€€ Al Bersagliere, *18 km northwest of Mantua in Goito, on SS236, T0376-60007*. While Goito is a cute hamlet, the main reason to come here is to try the cuisine at Al Bersagliere – and you won't be sorry. If their amazing *tortelli di zucca* or the equally stunning *agnolini* in capon broth is on you'll be happy. Follow them up with one of their game or fish main courses and you'll be in heaven. Well worth the diversion.

€€€€ Ambasciata, *30 km southeast of Mantua in Quistello, via Martiri di Belfiore 33, T0376-619169, ristoranteambasciata.com*. Foodies and critics love Ambasciata, not just because the food is sublime (it is), but because there is a real sense of passion for food and life here. Romano Tamani might have two Michelin stars, but the elegance of his restaurant is underplayed by the quirkiness of an antique store in some of the decoration. Whatever you order make sure you try the pasta dishes – Tamani is a master pasta-maker.

€€€€ Dal Pescatore, *38 km west of Mantua in Canneto sull'Oglio, just off SS10, T0376-723001, dalpescatore.com*. For most diners, Michelin three-star restaurants are daunting and formal affairs, with stuffy waiters and sommeliers trying to steer you towards a bottle of something you'll need a second mortgage to pay off. Inspired by French country restaurants that Antonio Santini and his wife Nadia (now the main chef) saw on their honeymoon, this restaurant, located between Mantua and Cremona, has become the Italian equivalent of what they saw. The food is approachable, with plenty of the best *tortelli* (filled pasta) you will ever try, and their sea bass and duck dishes are legendary.

🎭 Entertainment

Mantua *p82*
Bars and clubs
Buca della Gabbia, *Via Cavour 98, T0376-366901*. This wine bar gets especially crowded and cosy on a winter's evening when it's a great place to warm the bones.
Tiratappi, *piazza Alberti 30, T376-322366*. Tucked away down a little laneway off Piazza Mantegna, right near Sant'Andrea church, this wonderful old wine bar has a loyal following who flock here for the local wines and short menu of tasty regional snacks.

Classical music, opera and theatre
The awe-inspiring **Palazzo Te** (via Giovanni Acerbi) plays host to performances and recitals of classical and other music but see the tourist office for details of events organised by other musical associations and sponsors, not the Palazzo itself.

🛍 Shopping

Mantua *p82*
Mantua's best shopping is to be found in the streets around piazza Broletto and piazza Erbe, and along corsos Umberto I and Vittorio Emanuele II. You'll find plenty of chic boutiques, shoes and accessories shops, along with gourmet food stores.

Clothing and accessories
Folli Follie, *Corso Vittorio Emanuele II 21-27, T0376-360390, follifollie.it*. Giuseppe and Lucia Galli opened their first Folli Follie store here in Mantova in 1970, and now own some seven stores across northern Italy, specialising in stylish Italian clothes, shoes and accessories.
Lubiam, *Viale Fiume 55, T039-376 3091, lubiam.it*. A favourite with fashion-conscious guys, this is the outlet store for one of Italy's most notable, and in recent years more stylish, men's labels, which has been in the business of making tailored suits since 1911.

⚙ What to do

Mantua *p82*
Boating
Several boat companies offer cruises on Mantua's placid lakes during the warmer months, but **Motonavi Andes Negrini** (via San Giorgio 2, T0376-322875, motonaviandes.it) is the most popular, offering several options of 60- or 90-minute cruises on Lago di Mezza, Lago Inferiore and Lago Vallazza, departing around eight times a day from its jetty on Lago Inferiore. From €8, book in advance.

Cycling
There are several sign-posted cycling routes around Mantua, a wonderful town to bike around. See the tourist office (piazza Mantenga 6, T0376-432432, turismo.mantova.it) for details. You can hire bikes from **Mantua Bike Di Busselli Giovanni** (viale Piave 22b, T0376-220 909) for €2 hour/€8 day.

⊖ Transport

Mantua *p82*
If you're arriving in Mantua from Padua or Ferrara on via Legnago, prepare to grab your camera. Mantua is breathtakingly

beautiful from this approach, its muscular castle appearing to float on the water. If you're coming from Lago di Garda, Brescia or Verona, the easiest access to the city is on via Mulini but it's worth going the extra distance and taking the Mantua Nord exit from the A22 simply to enjoy the jaw-dropping views of the city. While there's plenty of parking all over the city, there's nowhere to pull over as you come across the causeway between Lago Inferiore and Lago di Mezzo, so have your camera ready and slow down.

Contents

Background

History

Roman Veneto

Veneto was populated by various tribes, including the Veneto Eugeni, the Rhaetians and the Veneti around the sixth century BC. They settled near the lagoon and on the banks and tributaries of the Adige and Brenta rivers. The people who located here had migrated from numerous territories, including Greece (some Venetians still consider themselves to be descendents of Troy), Gaul and Illyria. Scientists recently carried out tests on the people of Posina, a small village near Vicenza, and those from Barco di Pravisdomini, a village near the lagoon. These people look the same, speak the same dialect and would both consider themselves as indigenous but they have totally different mitochondrial DNA. This is highly unusual and shows the ethnic melting pot that Veneto once was.

Around 300 BC the Romans came, saw and conquered Veneto. Romanization of the area was completed in 89 BC when the cities of Tritium (Treviso), Patavium (Padua), Vincentia (Vicenza) and Verona became *municipia* and their male inhabitants were made Roman citizens, with the right to vote, stand for office, make binding contracts including those with foreigners, get married, move around the Roman Empire and enjoy a host of civil liberties. Roman mercantile tradition encouraged great prosperity in Veneto. The saying, *'omnes vias pecuniae norunt'* (they know all the ways of money) is most often said of the Venetians but was true of all those living in this thriving region.

The ambition and wealth of the Roman Empire can best be seen in Verona. The city was a strategic gateway to the Alps and lay between the key Roman cities of Genoa and Aquileia. Its humungous Arena (see page 21), built in AD 30, is one of the three best preserved amphitheatres in Italy (behind the Coliseum and the arena in Capua) and the only one that is still regularly used for performances. The Roman *decumanus* grid layout of the streets is still apparent in the modern city and the ruins of the Forum, conduits and other Roman buildings are visible under your feet. Verona's Teatro Romano (see page 26), built in the first century BC, is less complete than the Arena. However, the Museo Archeologico has a model of the theatre that reveals its original size and splendour.

The region also fathered two of the Roman era's most famous writers. Gaius Valerius Catullus, playboy, author of erotic poetry and inspiration to Ovid and Virgil, was born in Verona in 84 BC. Some 25 years later Livy (Titus Livius) was born in Padua and, after moving to Augustus, wrote *Ab Urbe Condita* (From the Founding of the City), one of the definitive texts on the history of Rome.

Christianity was awarded official status in the Roman Empire by Emperor Constantine in AD 313. The creation of a state religion and the recognition of a more absolute, natural law above that of the state and its figureheads is considered by some to be the beginning of the end of the Roman Empire. What's more, the increasing urbanization of the Empire through the building of fortified cities meant that peripheral areas were constantly at risk of attack by barbarians. Unprotected by Roman leagues, who were focused on progressing their eastern boundaries, these areas became depopulated and Rome's grasp on many parts of its empire started to weaken. In AD 331 Constantinople became capital of the Roman Empire and, over the following decades, power shifted eastwards. The fifth century saw the Visigoths and Ostrogoths making significant gains in the northern territories, including Veneto, which was taken by Theodoric the Ostrogoth in AD 489. Rome had fallen a few years earlier in AD 476, when Romulus Augustus, the last Roman Emperor, was displaced by Odoacer, a Germanic barbarian. This signalled the end of the Roman Empire and classical antiquity and the beginning of the Middle Ages and the Byzantine Empire.

The rise of Venice and the Golden Age

It was the marauding barbarians who ran amok in Veneto in the fourth and fifth centuries who provided the catalyst for the creation of Venice. Refugees, fleeing the violence and chaos, headed to the islands of the Venetian lagoon, which provided a safe, naturally defended haven. The first settlements were rough wooden huts suspended on stilts, which were built on some of the myriad marshy mudflats. The supposed date for the founding of Venice was 25 April 412 (St Mark's Day) but there is no real evidence to support this.

Attila the Hun is known to have plundered Veneto in AD 452 (a stone chair, alleged to be his throne, can be seen at Torcello), followed by Totial the Goth in AD 552 and then the Lombards in AD 570. Each successive incursion saw ever greater numbers of people migrating to the lagoon. By the seventh century AD Venice's major settlements were Heraclea (now Cittanova), on the mainland coast of the lagoon, Malamocco on the Lido, which had direct access to the Adriatic, Olivolo (now the Sant'Elena area of Castello) and the more sheltered Rivo Alto (which became Rialto). It is claimed that Venice's first doge, Paoluccio Anafesta, was elected in AD 697 and ruled from Heraclea, although the first officially recorded doge was Orso Ipato in AD 726 whose seat was Malamocco. As the population increased, so did Venice's status. In AD 776, Olivolo was awarded a bishop's seat by the Pope on the site of San Pietro.

Around this time Venice found itself caught up in the scuffles between the Eastern Byzantine Empire (ruled by Nicephorus) and the Western Empire (ruled by Charlemagne). Charlemagne's son, Pepin, seized Chioggia and Palestrina in AD 810 and was only kept out of the Venetian settlement by the narrow channel of water between the mainland and Malamocco. After this close call, Venice's administrative functions and many of its noble families moved to the Rivo Alto area, thus consolidating the city. It quickly developed a distinct identity and, significantly, a maritime presence.

In AD 828, two Venetian merchants stole the body of St Mark from Alexandria and took it back to Venice. Doge Giustiniano Participazio was delighted: securing the relics of such a significant Apostle was a major boon for the city, giving it a divine status and ensuring a constant stream of paying pilgrims. Within four years the first basilica in San Marco had been built. This burned down in 976 but was rebuilt soon after and consecrated in 1094.

The first symbolic marriage of the city to the sea took place in 1000 with Doge Pietro Orseolo taking the vows in a tradition that continues to this day on the festival of La Sensa. Venice's location, its growing population and its maritime dominance contributed to the city's niche as a trading post between East and West. As trade grew so did Venice's interest in affairs beyond the lagoon. Venice sought the assistance of Constantinople to deal with Slavic pirates who pestered and plundered the goods on Venetian ships working the Mediterranean. In return, Venice lent its support against Muslim Saracen forces that were seeking to conquer strategic positions in the eastern Mediterranean. A number of Venetian ships were involved in the First Crusade in 1095, although this was not a political intervention but a private venture by merchants who sought to curry favour and protect their trading routes.

Meanwhile, more of the lagoon's marshland was drained and cultivated or developed as the city expanded. Huge logs, 7.5 m long, were forced into the sandy clay then packed with stone from Padua or elsewhere in the region before stone foundations were laid. Single storey houses with courtyards were typical of the age, with wells dug into them for drinking water. Bridges were built over the network of canals. In 1171 the six *sestieri* of San Marco, Castello (formerly Olivolo), Cannaregio, San Polo, Santa Croce and Dorsoduro were created for administrative purposes and, in 1173, the first Rialto Bridge was erected. This was of wooden construction with a drawbridge in the middle to allow sailboats to pass through. The city also began to enjoy its position as the well-paid middleman in the trade of silks, spices and jewels.

Venice helped in the Fourth Crusade (1199-1204) and was able to expand its territory into Dalmatia and Corfu. As Constantinople's power crumbled away, Venice took control of trading routes in Asia and the Far East and Doge Enrico Dandolo was given the catchy title of 'Lord of a Quarter and a Half Quarter of the Empire'. Four bronze horses were taken as booty from the Hippodrome in Constantinople and flaunted on the roof of the Basilica San Marco.

In 1295 Marco Polo returned after 17 years in China (and seven years travelling there and back) laden with gems and stories of exotic lands and treasures. The taste for Eastern pleasures became something of a hobby amongst the Venetian nobility, as artefacts in both the Museo Storico Navale and the Museo Orientale at Ca' Pesaro bear out. By this time, Venice had transformed itself into a rich, influential city, protected by its natural boundaries. There seemed no end to its desire for wealth and supremacy. Furthermore, it wasn't prepared to share its power or influence with anyone.

The late 13th and early 14th century saw a number of moves by Venice's ruling class to entrench their privileged position and to ensure that the title of Doge was restricted to just a few families. In 1297 membership of the Greater Council was made permanent and hereditary. The building of Palazzo Ducale began in 1309, followed a year later by the creation of the Council of Ten. The council was established specifically to deal with an attempt to overthrow the Doge and was intended to provide greater security for the Republic's administration but it soon ended up running all of the Republic's diplomatic and military affairs, passing laws and managing the intelligence services, which sought to thwart rebellion or corruption. The compilation of the *Libro d'Oro* (Golden Book) in 1325, an official list of the Venetian nobility, determined who could vote or hold office in the Republic. No matter how rich and successful they became, those Venetians who weren't on the list could not break through this impregnable, if extravagantly gilded, glass ceiling. However, in later years, as the costs of constantly going to war mounted, it became possible to buy your way in to the Venetian nobility – for a hefty price, of course.

In 1308 the pope threatened to excommunicate Venice, following the Republic's attempt to snatch the river Po from Papal Ferrara. This irritated the Venetian authorities who didn't like the church interfering in its affairs. However, the biggest threat to Venice's dominance came in 1348-9 when the plague, supposedly brought by boats carrying Middle Eastern goods, ravaged the city. Almost 80,000 lives were lost: more than half the population. This had a terrible effect on the navy which, without Venetian men to enlist, had to hire mercenaries from Greece and Dalmatia who were not necessarily loyal to the Republic. Frequent scuffles with Genoa over trade culminated in the 1380 Battle of Chioggia at which the Republic regained control of the Adriatic, at least for a while.

As the challenge to Venice's domination of the seas increased, the Republic looked landwards to see how it could augment its power. In 1339 Venice had seized Treviso from the powerful Scaligeri family (see page 23). It took Vicenza in 1404 and Verona a year later, along with Padua from the Carraresis family. This expansion into terra firma encouraged noble families to build villas in the Veneto, famously along the Brenta Canal, but also in the fertile hinterland, where they sought to cultivate profits from agriculture. This proved to be a canny move by the Venetians. The loss of Constantinople to the Turks in 1453 and the discovery of the New World by the Portuguese at the end of the 1400s shifted maritime power away from Venice. And, as the world's focus turned to the west, the value of spices, for so long a cash cow for the Venetians, dropped.

The Renaissance

The 1500s marked the beginning of the decline of Venice's naval and trading dominance but you would never have known it. The Renaissance took hold of 'La Serenissima' – as the Republic's government rather vaingloriously called itself – and the city flourished like never before. The spread of new ideas in art and literature was facilitated by the advent of printing, which allowed for the production of small, portable books. The first printing press in Venice was set up by Teobaldo Mannucci (also known as Aldus Manutius), who published *Hypnerotomachia Poliphili* by a Dominican monk, Francesco Colonna, in 1499.

Venice's ambition and dedication to beauty created a fertile ground for artists such as Bellini, Titian and Tintoretto who imbued painting with realism, feeling and colour. But Venice struggled a little with new architectural ideas. While Vicenza, the home of Andrea Palladio, was sold on the new classicism, Venice took time to let go of the old and fuddled Gothic and to sign up to the new precise and intellectual style. However, by this time, the city needed better infrastructure to support its large population, which was bigger than Rome's and Florence's put together, and the nobility were keen to display their growing power and wealth in grand building projects. Jacopo Sansovino (1486-1570) was employed as the city's *Proto* (chief architect) and set about restyling piazza San Marco. Palladio, meanwhile, was commissioned to design the façade of San Francesco della Vigna in 1572. Renaissance architecture in Venice triumphed with the completion of Palladio's San Giorgio Maggiore in 1580.

Venice came under increasing foreign pressure during the 16th century. The League of Cambrai saw Pope Julius II, the Holy Roman Emperor, France and Spain joining forces to limit Venetian influence in northern Italy. Although the Pope later switched sides, the continued external threat created instability within the city, causing the Republic to turn in on itself. One of Venice's least glorious legacies was the creation of the Jewish ghetto in 1516. Although the persecution of the Jewish people was commonplace in Europe at that time, herding them into a designated area, restricting their movements and making them pay for the administration of such a policy was a new approach. The authorities became increasingly suspicious of internal conflict, establishing the State Inquisitors in 1540, who spied on prominent members of the ruling classes in an attempt to uncover plots and treachery. The state also sought to control the behaviour of its citizens. A series of laws were introduced between 1460 and 1543 to regulate prostitution, going so far as to stipulate what a prostitute could and couldn't wear, so that members of the public could distinguish a lady from a lady of the night. The Venetian Sumptuary Laws, passed in 1515 and 1562, prohibited displays of wealth and ostentation and even determined how much fish could be served at a banquet.

Vice, sodomy and the flaunting of riches were considered by the sanctimonious to be the cause of Venice's plague of 1575, when it lost one quarter of its population (50,000 people). So prolonged and dreadful was the experience that Pope Gregory XIII revoked all the Vatican's interdicts against the Republic. In 1577 the authorities agreed to build

Il Redentore to mark the end of plague and Palladio was commissioned to design it. However, this did not prevent the plague from striking again in 1630, in turn spurring the building of Santa Maria della Salute by Baldassare Longhena. In 1591 another iconic Venetian structure was built: the ponte di Rialto, designed by Andrea da Ponte.

Decline and fall

In 1669 Crete fell to the Turks and in 1718 the surrender of Morea was the last nail in the coffin of Venice's maritime empire. The Republic had no significant trading power and lost its *stato da mar*. However, back home, the Venetians were still having a rare old time. Vivaldi, Brunello and Goldoni were the showbiz names of the age. In 1703, Antonio Vivaldi became choirmaster of Ospedale della Pietà, an orphanage and music school for abandoned and deformed children. Recitals were held to fund the good works and many of the children went on to become accomplished musicians, even if they did have to play behind a grille so as to not offend the audience. Caffè Florian, with its resident orchestra, opened in 1720, filling piazza di San Marco with melody, followed in 1755 by Caffè Quadri. And, in 1790, La Fenice staged its first opera.

It was around this time that gambling became commonplace in the city, with fortunes and palazzi regularly changing hands. Excess was the order of the day and any excuse for revelry and feasting was indulged to the full. In 1725 Venice's most decadent and immoral ambassador, Giacomo Girolamo Casanova was born. After a stint at Padua University and a failed attempt at a monkish existence, he took to writing. He famously caroused, gambled, swindled, amused and seduced his way around the *calli* of the city, before being sent to jail in 1755. He escaped, of course, and fled to France, where he did more of the same on an international scale. The Venetian authorities eventually pardoned him and allowed him to return but, despite his celebrity status, he was poor and had to work as a lowly spy for the state just to get by. He fell foul of the authorities after mocking a member of the nobility and fled to Bohemia where he worked as a librarian for Count Joseph Karl von Waldstein until his death in 1798.

Revolution in France sent shockwaves around the European ruling elite. Initially, the ripples weren't noticed in Venice, a city that still believed in its own pre-eminence. However, when Napoleon, at war with Austria, began to encroach on Italian territories in 1797, Venice had to take notice. Napoleon took Verona, Vicenza, Padua and Mestre in quick succession and the fall of Venice became inevitable. On the 12 May 1797 Doge Ludovico Manin resigned and power was transferred to Napoleon. The French sailed into Venice a few days later, selected the treasure they wanted, then handed the city over to the Austrians. The Republic of Venice was at an end. Napoleon briefly sought to retake Venice to complete his portfolio as King of Italy but the Congress of Vienna in 1814-15 returned it to Austria's rule. The Venetians, at first bewildered by the turn of events, soon developed a simmering resolve to seize back control of their city.

The 19th and 20th centuries

In the 1800s the rest of the world finally caught on to Venice's treasures and it developed a reputation as a good-time city for monied visitors who sought a cultural haven like no other. Lord Byron came to Venice in 1818, staying with a menagerie of pets at Palazzo Mocenigo and using the library at San Lazzaro degli Armeni. Robert Browning bought a house in Asolo before returning to Venice to visit his son at Ca' Rezzonico, where he died in 1889. John Ruskin visited with his new wife Effie in 1848 and wrote *The Stones of Venice* while staying at the Palazzo Gritti. Henry James came in 1869 and set his 1902 novel *The Wings of the Dove* in the city. Richard Wagner visited many times in his life before dying of a heart attack in Palazzo Vendramin in 1883. Venice's status as a tourist destination was facilitated by the opening of the railway bridge to the mainland in 1846. This hugely controversial development turned the once independent state into a mere peninsula of mainland Italy.

Veneto's resentment towards its Austrian rulers turned to revolt in 1848 with uprisings across the region, most significantly in Padua. The resistance surrendered the following year and the Risorgimento's student leaders in Padua were hanged. However, the Second War of Independence in 1859 showed more promise, with Giuseppe Garibaldi garnering popular support across the country. In 1866 the Third Italian War saw the liberation of Venice and Veneto from Austrian rule. Venice didn't go back to being an independent Republic, however, but instead became part of a unified nation.

At the turn of the 20th century, Venice's popularity among foreign visitors was augmented by the development of the Lido as a chic seaside resort and by the staging of the first Venice Biennale showcasing international contemporary art. However, the advent of World War I saw the region once more at war with Austria, with bombing raids across Veneto. The Alpini regiment of the Italian army fought the fiercest battles in the Dolomites and around Monte Grappa. Post-war humiliation and the economic collapse that ensued led to the rise of Italian nationalism. Benito Mussolini gained power in 1923 and Italy became a Fascist state.

At the start of World War II, Italy was an ally of Nazi Germany: the Jews of Veneto were sent to concentration camps and many cities in the region were shelled by Allied forces, with Padua, Treviso and Verona suffering the most; Venice was let off lightly. However, in July 1943 the Italian government withdrew its support for Mussolini and, on 8th September, an armistice was signed between Italy and the Allies. The Italian army began to fragment: some soldiers remained Fascists and continued to support the Germans who occupied the north of Italy; some went into hiding but many others became partisans, fighting against the Fascists and the Nazis. Mussolini was shot by partisans while attempting to flee the country in April 1945.

The end of the war signalled a new beginning for Veneto, which was transformed from Italy's second poorest region to one of the most agriculturally and industrially rich in the country. However, the intensification of industry around the Venetian lagoon at Marghera and increased levels of water traffic were contributing factors in the devastating floods experienced by Venice in 1966, which spoiled artworks and damaged buildings. The clean-up continued well into the 1970s, with international organizations such as Save Venice and Venice in Peril set up to raise funds. The floods had another unforeseen effect: thousands of Venetians, unwilling to suffer the increasingly high tides, moved to the mainland town of Mestre. The impact of heavy industry, the depopulation of the city and the deluge of tourists who descend on this floating island each year continue to put Venice's very existence at risk.

Contents

Footnotes

Menu reader

General

affumicato smoked
al sangue rare
alla griglia grilled
antipasto starter/appetizer
aperto/chiuso open/closed
arrosto roasted
ben cotto well done
bollito boiled
caldo hot
cameriere/cameriera waiter/waitress
conto the bill
contorni side dishes
coperto cover charge
coppa/cono cone/cup
cotto cooked
cottura media medium
crudo raw
degustazione tasting menu of several dishes
dolce dessert
fatto in casa homemade
forno a legna wood-fired oven
freddo cold
fresco fresh, uncooked
fritto fried
menu turistico tourist menu
piccante spicy
prenotazione reservation
primo first course
ripieno a stuffing or something that is stuffed

secondo second course

Drinks (*bevande*)

acqua naturale/gassata/frizzante still/sparkling water
aperitivo drinks taken before dinner, often served
  with free snacks
bicchiere glass
birra beer
birra alla spina draught beer
bottiglia bottle
caffè coffee (ie espresso)
caffè macchiato/ristretto espresso with a dash of
  foamed milk/strong
spremuta freshly squeezed fruit juice
succo juice
vino bianco/rosato/rosso white–rosé/red wine

Fruit (*frutta*) and vegetables (*legumi*)

agrumi citrus fruits
amarena sour cherry
arancia orange
carciofio globe artichoke
castagne chestnuts
cipolle onions

cocomero water melon
contorno side dish, usually grilled vegetables or
  oven-baked potatoes
fichi figs
finocchio fennel
fragole strawberries
friarelli strong flavoured leaves of the broccoli
  family eaten with sausages
frutta fresca fresh fruit
funghi mushroom
lamponi raspberries
melagrana pomegranate
melanzana eggplant/aubergine
melone light coloured melon
mele apples
noci/nocciole walnuts/hazelnuts
patate potatoes, which can be *arroste* (roast),
  fritte (fried), *novelle* (new), *pure' di* (mashed)
patatine fritte chips
peperoncino chilli pepper
peperone peppers
pesche peaches
piselli peas
pomodoro tomato
rucola rocket
scarola leafy green vegetable used in torta di scarola pie.
sciurilli or *fiorilli* tempura courgette flowers
spinaci spinach
verdure vegetables
zucca pumpkin

Meat (*carne*)

affettati misti mixed cured meat
agnello lamb
bistecca beef steak
bresaola thinly-sliced, air-cured beef from Valtellina
carpaccio finely sliced raw meat (usually beef)
cinghiale boar
coda alla vaccinara oxtail
coniglio rabbit
involtini thinly sliced meat, rolled and stuffed
manzo beef
pollo chicken
polpette meatballs
polpettone meat loaf
porchetta roasted whole suckling pig
prosciutto ham – *cotto* cooked, *crudo* cured
salsicce pork sausage
salumi cured meats, usually served mixed
  (*salumi misto*) on a wooden platter
speck a type of cured, smoked ham
spiedini meat pieces grilled on a skewer
stufato meat stew
trippa tripe
vitello veal

Fish (*pesce*) and seafood (*frutti di mare*)

acciughe anchovies
aragosta lobster
baccalà salt cod
bottarga mullet-roe
branzino sea bass
calamari squid
cozze mussels
frittura di mare/frittura di paranza small fish, squid and
  shellfish lightly covered with flour and fried
frutti di mare seafood
gamberi shrimps/prawns
grigliata mista di pesce mixed grilled fish
orata gilt-head/sea bream
ostriche oysters
pesce spada swordfish
polpo octopus
sarde, sardine sardines
seppia cuttlefish
sogliola sole
spigola bass
stoccafisso stockfish
tonno tuna
triglia red mullet
trota trout
vongole clams

Dessert (*dolce*)

cornetto sweet croissant
crema custard
dolce dessert
gelato ice cream
granita flavoured crushed ice
macedonia (di frutta) fruit cocktail dessert with white wine
panettone type of fruit bread eaten at Christmas
semifreddo a partially frozen dessert
sorbetto sorbet
tiramisù rich 'pick-me-up' dessert
torta cake
zabaglione whipped egg yolks flavoured with
  Marsala wine
zuppa inglese English-style trifle

Other

aceto balsamico balsamic vinegar, usually from Modena
arborio type of rice used to make risotto
burro butter
calzone pizza dough rolled with the chef's choice of
  filling and then baked
casatiello lard bread
fagioli white beans
formaggi misti mixed cheese plate
formaggio cheese
frittata omelette

insalata salad
insalata Caprese salad of tomatoes, mozzarella
  and basil
latte milk
lenticchie lentils
mandorla almond
miele honey
olio oil
polenta cornmeal
pane bread
pane-integrale brown bread
pinoli pine nuts
provola cheese, sometimes with a smoky flavour
ragù a meaty sauce or ragout
riso rice
salsa sauce
sugo sauce or gravy
zuppa soup

Useful phrases

posso avere il conto per favore? can I have the bill please?
c'è un menù? is there a menu?
che cosa mi consegna? what do you recommend?
cos'è questo? what's this?
dov'è il bagno? where's the toilet?

Index → *Entries in bold refer to maps.*